THE SECOND REPUBLIC

By

NORMAN A. SAX

Dedicated to 45

Introduction

I was born in a failed state. Over the course of my lifetime, I have seen institution after institution fall into the hands of the few, insulated from the many. Those few have no lover for my country, or for any country. They love only their own class, held above national allegiance and loyalty to those who they once claimed to serve. These institutions now serve neither their own stated goals, nor the people in general. They exist only to acquire, maintain and use power. The institutions and the people who control them treat us as chattel; batteries to power their global machine, detrimental to the vast swathes of humanity.

Perhaps it was always so. Perhaps the elite classes never cared for the little people. Perhaps we have always been serfs on the plantation of the world. But when these elites were close to the people in culture and proximity, it didn't matter much, We could exert our control over them to a sufficient degree to keep our lives our own.

In a final stroke, the illusion of consent has been stripped away from the regime in my country; and when artifice fails, only brute force remains. At the time of this writing, my former country has been occupied by a foreign Communist government. We are no longer sovereign. Not even our illiberal rulers, camped behind barbed wire in their alabaster city, are sovereign. We are vassals and slaves to the most disgusting and murderous regime in human history.

It happened without a single tank; it happened without a moment of recognition. In the middle of the night on 7 January 2021, a compact was formalized by our illiberal regime to hand total power to our most hated enemy. It happened without fully awakening the sleeping giant.

And at the time of this writing, most of my countrymen sleep still.

How did this happen?

By 1920, my country's regime, as defined in our written Constitution, had been amended in three ways that provided a pathway for the national government to control the several regional governments, and then the people, rather than the other way around. Our national character transitioned from an acquisition and conquest footing of a free and muscular people to an acquisition and distribution footing of a sclerotic and declining one. By 1965, our governance had changed so drastically that our leaders sold our birthright to every man on Earth willing to fill out his claim to our bounty. In this generation, there is no need for even that: our rulers openly court invasion by anyone who can reach our shores.

Here, now, we are seeing the first inklings of genocide. The process really began in earnest in the 1970s on the heels of the domestic civil rights movement. Communists took control of the schools that year or thereabouts. We are now three or more generations of teachers from that turning point. Modern teachers teach Marxism in modern schools to modern children who only learn Marxism, and therefore cannot think the way a free people must. In these past years the pace has been quickening. For how does a culture fail? Slowly at first, then all at once.

First we heard about affirmative action, and then diversity, and then multiculturalism. And then the mass marketing of homosexuality and transgenderism and now pedophilia. And then the denigration of white history and the obliteration of the markers of the same; All the while seeing the very worst of anti-whiteness lionized and protected by our government at the expense of the whole of the people of all colors and of our traditions.

Pogroms in the street have started with the blessing of the ruling class both without and within the government. Paramilitary forces burn cities and destroy businesses. They attack homeowners and those who would band together to defend their lives and property by force. We who fight back in word and deed are demonized, labeled terrorists, and locked up as political prisoners.

Our government has done this because they know that only the traditional stakeholders in our native land are capable of, and care enough to put up a fight. We were the last of them to continue our objection to their rulership, and we have been demonized for it.

This country is lost; perhaps for the next 100 years. With the dawning of the Information Age a generation ago, elites have ever-greater tools for totalitarian control. It may take much longer than times past for the world to see another sun rise in liberty.

Those who still have passion, rhetoric, and meager firearms will naturally look to fight back against an unjust state. They remember the state that was and wish for it to return. From war there is no homecoming. No man returns to woman as the same man as he left. Perhaps they do not know.

Even today, the worst crime a man can commit is to name the people responsible for our national destruction, and so I will not name them. But you know who they are, or you soon will.

In the meantime we must, as our ancestors have done, strike out to find new lands to forge to a new nation for a people as ancient as Humanity itself. And in this monumental effort, we must ensure that those attacks which brought us low shall not have such an easy time of it as they did in the homeland of my birth; not for us, but for our nation and our progeny down through generations.

The world must always have a beacon of liberty to aspire to; a forward-looking nation which grasps for greatness; men who build great works through honest labor and God's gifts of natural resource and of intellect; men who will be called upon to save the world again, and very soon.

This work is our blueprint for that new nation, under God, indivisible, with liberty and justice for all. We call this land the Second Republic.

Paper One. General Notes.

Part I. Preamble.

No human society is perfect. Each of them is made up of people, who are imperfect and imperfectable. Human nature is immutable and therefore no perfect man will be born, except another sent by God. Like human beings, societies grow and experiment, and then decline and die. It has always been this way and it will always be this way for as long as there are people.

However, we also see peoples and cultures which endure, and ideas which prove useful time and again. It is the goal of these papers to define a second republic more perfect than the first, to be enacted on this globe, at some future time and in some way.

A Republic is more than a constitution, whether it's written or not. It's more than families and the aspirations of the sovereign people. It's more than its government which operates by that constitution. It is more than its businesses and their corporate branding.

Throughout these papers, we will define aspects of a society and culture and the regime and government those people will enact. We will proceed step-wise from the smallest elements of such a republic to the largest ones, touching on each of them just enough to ensure agreement on our definitions and our aims. Ultimately we will devise a written constitution and other markers of statehood including a national church, a national flag, a declaration of liberty from the old republic and a pledge of citizenship[1].

Finishing where we started Part I, consider again that no society is perfect. You will see ideas presented that you will disagree with; but each idea presented is here for a reason. Please give each one its due, both individually and in the whole. Many of the definitions and explanations will seem to be limiting, especially to a man who has been raised to love liberty and the rights promised to him by God. However in the whole, we will see that the limits we place will lead to greater liberty and better harmony with God than we have had before. This is a blueprint for both a culture and for a country, and the prohibitions herein will provide synergy between the two, which will lead those men who enact it to great personal wellbeing.

Let's begin.

---

[1] Some of which appear in this document; others do not.

Part II. Definitions.

First things first: the reader should endeavor to use the same definitions of words we use to the best of his ability. If you are reading this text a long time from when it was written, please take care to understand what this generation of men meant with the words we used, both individually and in idiom. Language evolves over time. Sometimes over a very short time, like what's happening in our time, today. But the *meaning* of the language is immutable. Therefore we expect the reader to do his part to ensure fidelity of cold fact and passionate nuance when translating our language into yours.

Let's start small and work our way up, like a ladder.

What is a Person? A Person is any human living or dead. Personhood begins at conception and lasts in perpetuity. Nothing else besides a human can be a person, be it animal, vegetable, mineral, or anything else.

All Persons are equal before the Law and before God. In this imperfect Realm, persons are all unique, and each has his own strengths and weaknesses. In short, Nature makes each person different than the next.

All Persons have several inalienable physical qualities which are evident and useful. Here are the two most important immutable physical characteristics useful for classifying Persons.

- In every case, **a Person is immutably a Man or a Woman only,** defined at conception, and positively identified at birth or before based solely on his chromosomes.
- In every case, **a Person's race is immutable,** defined at conception, and identified at birth or before by that person's immutable phenotype or phenotypes. No later alteration to this designation is possible. Persons of every race are human.

What is a Citizen?

Now that we have defined Persons and their fundamental natural interrelations, we can define the Citizen. Recall that these shall be legally-binding definitions.

A **Citizen** is a Person whose Parents are both citizens, or a Person who has gone through a stringent legal test of cultural compatibility and economic value to the Republic and has subsequently been naturalized and granted permanent citizenship. The responsibilities and benefits of Citizenship shall be defined elsewhere and by statute as required.

A Citizen will owe his national allegiance to the Republic and strive to advance her power relative to other states; and the Republic shall in all events put the welfare of a Citizen above that of any other Person.

A Citizen shall not at any time possess **dual citizenship**. In order to be a Citizen, a Person must forsake all other national allegiance in perpetuity. If a Person accepts citizenship in any other state, Citizenship in the Republic is immediately and irreversibly revoked.

Only Citizens shall be permanent residents of the Republic.

What is a Family? A Family is a number of people larger than one related primarily through marriage or blood. People naturally form families. This is inherent to the nature of Mankind.

While God has endowed each *Person* with the inalienable rights of life, liberty and the pursuit of wealth among many other things, **the indivisible unit of the Republic is the Family.** Families sustain and propagate the Republic; an individual cannot do it alone. It is for this reason the Republic shall grant special status to the **Family**, the nature of which we will talk about later.

What are Parents? Parents are members of a family legally responsible for the welfare of minor children, some number of which are blood relatives (descendants.) A maximum of one man and one woman may be legally designated as the parents of a person.

What is Marriage? Marriage is a **contract**. It is not a right, nor is it a responsibility of any man or woman. This contract exists primarily **to maintain family stability** in order to provide the best probability **for producing children** and raising them to be valuable citizens.

Again: Marriage is a contract and exists primarily for the benefit of the children of the married persons and for the state.

For reasons we will cover later, marriages, once consummated, shall exist in perpetuity, even beyond death. There will be limited cases where divorce or annulment is permissible, but these cases will be grave and be rare.

What is a Republic? A **Republic** is an indivisible polity, within which the supreme authority, or sovereignty, rests within the entirety of the citizenry rather than in a single individual, the military, some guild or some religious group, or some external authority entirely. While we take "Republic" to have a positive connotation, it is just as likely that a Republic can be founded by evil men for evil means as for good men to found one for purposes we take to be good.

Part III: The State, The Nation, This Republic

What is A State?

A State is a legal entity that satisfies basic requirements. These are the bare minimum requirements for an entity to qualify as a State. They are:

- Maintains a Defined Territory;
- And Maintains a monopoly on the lawful use of deadly force within those borders.

What is a Nation?

A Nation is a single people,

- united by blood,
- united by a unitary culture,
- and united by shared sentiment of cooperation.

Sometimes a State and a Nation are concomitant; in other times they are not. One reason these two entities may not be concomitant is that the Nation has spread far and wide and resides in many host states; another is that the Nation has not developed sufficiently advanced culture and infrastructure to form a State.

Each of these structures is more or less stable on its own. We can see examples of several States and several Nations existing for hundreds or thousands of years. However, the strongest and most longstanding polities are those which combine the qualities of both to have a State and a Nation exist together in harmony.

What is The Second Republic?

We'll want a State and a Nation as a foundation upon which to build our Republic. Having defined the State and the Nation generally, let us now define what we mean when we refer specifically to the Second Republic.

The Second Republic is

- a legal entity that maintains a Defined Territory,
- maintains a monopoly on the lawful use of deadly force within those borders,
- is lawfully permanently inhabited by Citizens,
- who share a single culture grounded in a common religion and civic aspiration grounded in *explicitly Christian*[2] values and law,
- which holds the wellbeing and prosperity of its own citizens far above that of any other persons or people, and
- that uses a single language including but not limited to speech, writing, sign language and Braille, in all official business.

---

[2] We leave the definition of Christianity to other scholars for now.

Paper Two. Culture, and the Nature of the Second Republic.

Part I. Preamble.

As we have said, a **Republic** is an indivisible nation, within which the supreme authority, or sovereignty, rests within the entirety of the citizenry. Therefore, what *kind* of republic we shall make depends most critically on the kind of **Citizen** who shall inhabit it. And the kind of citizen who shall inhabit it is determined most critically by the **Culture** which surrounds and permeates him.

Part II. National Aesthetics.

Every state has its own *aesthetic*, which is a combination of these elements and yet greater than the sum of them all. Poland has a quality we could call *Polish* and the United States has a quality we could call *American*. It is a quality that is hard to fully describe and it is as indivisible from that state as is its people themselves.

However, in all of the elements which so sum for which Man has in his power to control, it is the qualities exhibited by the men of the nation themselves which are most powerful. While human nature is immutable and eternal, culture is specific, traditional, and taught by one generation of men to the next. Therefore the best place to affect the aesthetic of the nation is to define which cultural characteristics which men value and advance, and those which she abhors and forbids over time.

Specifically in our republic, we are looking to establish a culture which unites a people and knits it together. We shall seek both civic and religious unity. This will keep our republic strong practically and spiritually, buttressing it against attacks from without and tyranny from within.

A popular sentiment among free men in times past was *e pluribus unum*. While it was used by postmodernists[3] as a lever to divide a people into many smaller divisions, the original intent was for each person and each family to unite in the singular culture of a nation to create an unbreakable bulwark against such division.

---

[3] Postmodernism refers to any number of trends or movements which started c. 1860 as a reaction and rejection to the dogma, principles, practices or traditions which have built the Western and Christian world. These include Marxism and all its economic and cultural descendants such as communism, critical theory, brutalist architecture and any of the social sciences ending in –studies, among other practices. The purpose of postmodernism is to erase human nature and create a new kind of man with an inherent nature completely divorced from that which has been endowed within us by God.

Since we want to make our culture strong, we must first be able to identify and describe that will make it strong. We must describe those values and qualities which we wish the people in our new republic to possess. The sum total of these values and qualities are called culture.

Then we must name and define the institutions necessary for a republic, and define the qualities we want those institutions to have. These institutions must have as part of their mission the strengthening and transmission of the culture we've decided on.

Once we have done these things, we can start to decide on the kinds of laws we will need in order to keep things running the way we want them to run. These laws are not the specific statutes, but rather the blueprint for the machine of state. No document like this can foresee every little thing that people might want to make a law about, but we can provide a framework within which those laws can be made and applied.

Let's get some more definitions out of the way so we can start working on this part of the republic.

Part III. Definitions.

What is Culture?

First and Foremost, **Culture is application of labor or other means to improve good qualities in, or growth**, of a Nation and its people; as the *culture* of the mind; the *culture* of virtue. That is, **Culture is an active element. It is in motion.** It shapes, and is shaped by, the citizenry and institutions of the Republic.

A Culture is shared. It refers to the total range of activities and ideas of a group of people with shared traditions, which are transmitted and reinforced by members of the group.

Culture is a repository of the ideals of a Nation and its people. It is **the total of the inherited ideas, beliefs, values, and knowledge**, which constitute the shared bases of societal action.

We may also refer to culture the quality in a person or society that arises from a **concern for what is regarded as excellent** in arts, letters, manners, scholarly pursuits, etc. Citizens ought to be cultured in this sense.

Finally, culture refers to the **artistic and social pursuits, expression, and tastes valued** by a Nation, its people or class of people; as in the arts, manners, dress, etc.

What is Virtue?

Moral goodness; the practice of moral duties and the abstaining from vice, or a conformity of life and conversation to the moral law. In this sense, virtue may be, and in many instances must be, distinguished from religion. The practice of moral duties merely from motives of convenience, or from compulsion, or from regard to reputation, is *virtue* as distinct from religion. The practice of moral duties from sincere love to God and his laws, is *virtue*.

What is Good?

Good means possessing the qualities, whether they be moral, physical or intellectual, best adapted to its design and use, or the qualities which God's law requires: virtuous, pious, and religious applied to persons, and opposed to bad, vicious, wicked, and evil. Herein we refer to an explicitly Christian God.

When we talk about religions, we really mean "something like Christianity." Christianity is the only religion like Christianity. Other beliefs are *like* religions, but don't really fit the same definition. In common parlance, "religion" = "Christianity" but this is an incorrect formulation. No two belief systems we *call* religions are distinct flavors of the same thing, but each is rather a different thing entirely. There is some concomitance between religions, but they are not truly of a class with one another. Therefore each religion will have its own definition of vice and virtue, good and evil.

Part IV. The Virtuous Citizen.

Now that we have established that the Republic's character rests upon the character and virtue of its citizens, we must define which specific virtues we wish to instill in our citizenry[4].

We look to Aristotle to see the definition of the virtuous man. In fact, he describes such a man as a Hero, and this is an apt description.

A Hero has six primary virtues. They must be collected in this specific order, for each is built upon the foundation of the previous ones, like a pyramid.

Virtue One is to keep **Truth at the center of the mind**. This means that a man must always seek to know things as they are rather than how he wishes them to be. A man with truth at the center of his mind will prefer an abhorrent truth to a comforting lie.

Its corresponding Vice is **Narrativism**, which means that a man must first construct a worldview which pleases him, and then fit the

---

[4] *n.b.* These are *civic* virtues, which are similar to, but not the same as, *ecclesiastical* virtues. For those we shall defer to the Church.

facts to this narrative. Of all the Vices, this is the most poisonous to the mind.

Virtue Two is to practice **Right Reason**. This means that a man must believe that there is one true description of reality, and that he must apply his senses and intellect to discern what it is.

Its corresponding Vice is **Postmodernism**, which states there is no one correct frame of reference and that each opinion on reality is equally valid. Of all the Vices, this is the most poisonous to the Republic and must be fought against trenchantly at every Time and in every Place.

Virtue Three is **Prudence**. Prudence demands **caution of deliberation** on the most suitable means to accomplish valuable purposes, and the exercise of sagacity in discerning and selecting them. It differs from wisdom in that Prudence is more cautious and less spontaneous. Inalienable to Prudence is the saying, "First Do No Harm." Also inalienable is preparing for things which may go wrong (or go right) according to the application of the first two Virtues.

Its corresponding Vice is **Carelessness**. The misapplication of spontaneity results in negligence and harm. When a man is not instilled with discipline and responsibility he is prone to carelessness.

Virtue Four is **Justice**. Justice consists of giving every man his due. It pertains to men dealing with other men or to groups. In the case of the legal system of the Republic, it consists of the whole body of Citizens, at times of official legal conflict, bestowing upon each man what he is due.

Its corresponding Vice is **Fiat**, wherein a subject gives to an object what the subject desires to give, regardless of what the object deserves. While God has the power of Fiat, no man nor body of men shall practice it, for they are limited and have not the ability to marry Fiat to Justice. In God there are no irreconcilable contradictions, but this is not true for Men in this World.

Virtue Five is **Fortitude**. Fortitude is the ability to weather the physical, intellectual, emotional and moral strain of existence and to persevere in the face of adversity.

Its corresponding Vice is **Victimhood**, wherein a man attempts to achieve social, moral or other superiority over others by claiming prior injury at some other hand.

Virtue Six is **Temperance, which is the practice of moderation**; particularly habitual moderation in the indulgence of the several natural appetites and passions. Temperance also refers to moderation in the times and places where Justice shall be offered, for a man must know where to act and where to pause his actions in delivering outcome.

Its corresponding Vice is **Abandon**, wherein a man allows himself
to fall to a deadly sin when he could otherwise prevent it.

A man who achieves mastery of these six Virtues shall be
considered to have achieved the pinnacle of citizenship. Therefore
we shall construct our culture to transmit and lionize these virtues
and to defend against their corresponding vices in all matters.

Part V. Cultural Transmission.

Culture is both *taught* and it is *learned*. In both cases there are both
incidental and intentional transmission elements present. When
one hears a complaint that a particular group has no culture, what
that complaint means is that the transmission of the culture is
hidden from the plaintiff. And, in fact, if a man does not
concentrate on the transmission of culture, it can seem that nothing
is happening at all.

There exists constant cultural transmission from every source and
in every place; some intentional and some incidental. For he who is
not actively observing and pursuing this transmission, it will be lost
to him, even if he himself is the recipient.

Cultural Vectors.

Broadly, there are five primary intentional cultural vectors and a sixth incidental vector.

- The first vector both in sequence and in magnitude is the **Family**. Consider the infant, the son, the brother, the father, the patriarch. At the center of each of these rôles exists cultural transmission to other family members. Therefore the most important institution in our Republic shall be the Family, due in part to its central role in transmitting our culture from one man to the next.

- The second vector of cultural transmission is **Mass Media**. While there are closer and warmer cultural vectors, no force transmits culture more ubiquitously and with greater focus than the mass media, whether it is news or entertainment or advertisement or control of the online Public Square space. Without the firm hand of discipline, this vector may become controlled by a few men all drawn from a single class, and therefore allow these men to inflict tyrannical, yet invisible, harm to the culture. Therefore it is to this vector both Men individually and their Government shall pay the strictest attention and correct with most regularly, trenchantly, and harshly.

- The third vector of cultural transmission is the **School**.[5] It is here that young Citizens learn the masculine and feminine

---

[5] School is first covered in Paper Three.

civic duties they shall favor and perform, and for many children it will be the environment in which they spend the most time outside the home.

- The fourth vector of cultural transmission is the **Church**.[6] It is here Citizens shall learn to love and fear Almighty God and how to live a Godly life. Recall we named and defined the civic virtues; we shall name and describe the *ecclesiastical* virtues in Paper Three. Furthermore, a singular united religious experience shall knit our Republic closer together and defend against attacks from entities which practice a different religion or creed.

- The fifth vector of cultural transmission is **Trades and Professions**. As children spend most of their time outside the home at school, so adults who work at remunerative tasks shall spend a large amount of time "at work." Therefore it is incumbent upon the whole of the people to enforce upon each workplace an acceptable work environment which is in harmony with the people as a whole. However, as each of the several trades and professions require different skills and different standards, this standard shall be applied most loosely of all these standards.

- The sixth vector of cultural transmission is **Intransitive Demographic**. This is an incidental, or passive vector. How cultural cues and norms impact each Person shall vary based on his race, sex, age, and other factors over which he has no

---

[6] Likewise, Church is first covered in Paper Three.

control. We shall seek to minimize the care given to this vector and maximize our discipline over it. This is because we wish to forge a singular people with many individuals of *talent and gift* rather than celebrate individuals based on qualities they cannot control.

Paper Three. The Nature of Family.

Part I. Preamble.

Now we have named the several institutions of cultural significance, and defined the Family[7] and its constituents. The several institutions we have named are primarily institutions of transmitting *civic* virtues: Seeking Truth, Right Reason, Prudence, Justice, Fortitude and Temperance.

We shall spend more time thinking about **Family**. What is its purpose? How does the Republic serve family? And more importantly, how can a correct family serve the Republic?

Let's begin.

Part II. Ideal Family Structure.

We have defined Family thus: **A Family** is a number of people larger than one related primarily through marriage or blood.

---

[7] Paper One.

While God has endowed each *person* with the inalienable rights of life, liberty and the pursuit of wealth among many other things, **the indivisible unit of the Republic is the Family.** This is because families sustain and propagate the Republic; an individual cannot do it alone.

Therefore it is important to suggest and celebrate strong families. Those families which are strongest generally follow strongly traditional gender roles. The division of labor is traditional: women will preside over the labor of the home while men will preside over the labor in the world. While many families will not meet the ideal, it is a good goal to attain it and maintain it. We shall encourage people to aspire to it.

As God made man the master of his wife, and the Head of Household shall be primarily male; it is delegated to this man to discipline his family including his wife. The government shall leave it to this head of household to discipline his family as he sees fit.

Here is an abhorrent truth: it is the nature of women to connive and win through subtle deception that which men might win by force. One of the very worst parts of the postmodernist practice of feminism is to neuter the man's strong hand in maintaining order and discipline. As responsibility falls upon the shoulders of the man of the house, it is his duty to keep his family in line through whatever means are necessary.

A man striking his wife and children is distasteful; but those women and children who will not be ruled otherwise bring greater ruin to themselves and to their families.

The Head of Household is be responsible for establishing the family's relationship to the community, although he may delegate this responsibility to other members of his family on his own authority.

The responsibility of maintaining the home, the home economics and the child-rearing shall fall to the oldest woman of the family when possible. She has the authority to direct her husband and other family members to maintain the home in a manner she sees fit, subject to her husband's right of discipline. Additionally, the woman is responsible for teaching the children in the home prior to their time at School.

Thusly, the several tasks are divided between the sexes. Men maintain the family's relationship to the world and women maintain the internal domestic tranquility.

As people are free to make their own choices, these tasks may be delegated to others within the family or in the employ of the family; and not every family has the structure necessary to comply with these roles. However, these are the ideal relationships to establish.

Part III. Family Privileges.

Since families are the building blocks of the Republic, they deserve special privileges for which individuals do not qualify.

The one privilege that only families shall have is that of voting, and each family shall have one vote. We will discuss the specifics of the franchise in a later chapter, but single people shall never earn the right to vote. Other special privileges of families will be granted by statute, but the responsibility of voting will devolve solely on families.

Paper Four. The Nature of Mass Media.

Part I. Preamble.

Mass media, or the press, is the one institution most capable of interceding between men and interceding between men and their government. A pervasive and coherent media message serves as an invisible advertisement for a particular life and culture that can be quite different from the one we would naturally choose. Furthermore, as the press is naturally incendiary, it will inevitably set man against man if left unchecked. We shall allow freedom of the press only to the extent that it is not harmful to those who consume and participate in it. That's different from the prevailing opinion of the West that says the most important principle of a free press is that it remains free.

We have seen that there is no institution more capable of putting its thumb on the scale of public opinion than a concerted mass media. It has been clear in every Western country for decades and longer that the media, once controlled by those with aligned ideologies, are more powerful even than the sovereign people in directing their own government. Therefore we have decided to temper licentiousness with the firm hand of sovereign correction. The press must not be greater than the people it serves, nor should the entertainment delivered be at odds with the standards and culture of the people who are to consume it. Any sanction against a person for violating community norms or instigating discord shall fall more harshly on the owner of the particular press or media outlet than the recipient or participant. That is, ownership carries with it grave responsibility.

Part II. Definitions.

What is Mass Media? Mass Media is a vehicle or means of communication that transmits information from a source to a target public. Any media intended for the larger audience, and not a single person or small group, shall be called mass media. The categories now include, but are not limited to in the future, **electromagnetic spectrum broadcasting** (such as TV and radio), **digital communications** (websites, social media), **motion pictures, timely print media** (newspapers, magazines), and **permanent print media** (books, records, documents.)

It is characteristic of Mass Media, above and beyond its value to inform and entertain, that **it has an outsized power to influence society**; and is also influenced by the mores and tastes of the people in society. Therefore it is incumbent upon the Republic to closely watch and regulate this cultural dance.

At the time of this writing and for some time before, a small handful of like-minded individuals, different in many ways from the heritage families of the old republic, control nearly all content in both news and entertainment. Rather than mirror the society and culture they purportedly serve, instead they provide an all-pervasive advertisement for the society and culture the ruling class wishes the people to emulate.

This gradual and inexorable bending of the societal will has been and will continue to be a grave threat to the virtuous Christian man and the state he inhabits. It is a prime concern of our Republic to hold fast to the Mass Media to prevent it from suborning our ruin.

Part III. Limiting the Reach of Mass Media.

First, we will seek to **Limit Harmful Content** closely in order to prevent the spread of depredation and moral decay. An example of such a regulation may be found in the Hays Code, applied against early Hollywood; however, any such **Code derived from the stated Civic and Ecclesiastical Virtues**[8] is sufficient for consideration. There shall be exceptions for exceptional circumstance, but these exceptions shall be rare and of value to society rather than for conscupient reasons or material gain.

---

[8] See Appendix I.

Second, we will seek to ensure that **no entertainment is allowed to purport truth value that is not present**. There shall be no special carve-out for "journalists" or "news agencies" above or beyond basic liberty to convey content. We shall encourage at every opportunity citizens and other free men to continually judge the quality and veracity of provided content. In this way, we shall **Limit Authority.**

Third, we shall limit the share of any medium or media owned by owner (whether sole proprietor or group) to reach no more than 20% of persons in the Republic; or, in the case of unlimited reach, that there should be no fewer than five such owners. This is to ensure that it is difficult for any one point of view to completely crowd out others.

Additionally, if an owner has captured a full 20% of any one kind of media, it may not own any other. That is, the total market share held by a single owner shall not exceed 20%. Should an owner hold an 18% market share in one mass media, he may own only 2% of the market in the sum total of all others. In this way, we shall **Limit Trusts,** or the accumulation of media power into fewer and fewer hands.

Fourth, we shall strictly prohibit direct government solicitation by those with interests in the Mass Media. Any owner and/or its representative shall be prohibited from holding public office or giving material aid to any public official sufficient to influence policy. In this way, we shall seek to **Limit Regulatory Capture** of the law by Mass Media entities.

In these four ways, and possibly in other ways, we will keep a firm hand on runaway mass media and have it serve the people rather than control them.

Paper Five. The Nature of School

Part I. Preamble.

What is a School? A **School** is an institution where people learn to be more culturally cohesive and materially productive citizens. Those activities which do not contribute to these goals do not qualify as schooling and are not part of a school. A school shall not be defined by its size, place, or assets but rather by purpose.

School has three purposes, each as important as the other two.

- The first is to teach **proper socialization** among peers, inferiors and superiors.
- The second is to teach broad and deep **cultural knowledge**, which comes from our forebears.
- The third is to teach **practical skill** in those fields which are necessary for a person, family, community and the Republic to function.

Part II. Educational Philosophy.

The modern Western factory model of school has failed. It was designed to fail. It has been a long, costly, and disastrous social experiment which has destroyed the seed corn of cultural and practical excellence in several modern states. This model therefore must be rejected. A paradigm shift is vital in order to regain the dynamic strength our people once possessed. Just what the new school will look like and how pedagogy will change is up in the air. At the risk of sounding glib, we just can't keep doing what we're doing and expect it to work better next time.

Culture is a whole, and not a mosaic of many isolated parts; students will study elements of the culture as one might study a river, and not as one might study the motes it carries along. While the nuts and bolts of time and activity sometimes make each part of this study feel like a distinct subject, it is important for students to be able to assemble these various tranches into a cohesive whole.

In order to ensure that students are placed on the Hero's Path of civic virtue, **the positive study and advocacy for postmodernism in all its perditious forms shall be strictly prohibited and sanctioned in the strongest possible way.** The penalty for postmodernist advocacy shall be exile and the forfeiture of all wealth and property.

Part III. Appropriate Composition.

As we have said, a school is an institution where children and adults learn to be more culturally cohesive and materially productive citizens; and those activities which do not contribute to these goals do not qualify as schooling and are not part of a school.

Pupils shall enter school for the first time during the calendar year which they turn 8 years old. They shall immediately take an entrance exam to determine their placement. Such exams shall be administered every two years (age 10, 12, etc.) to determine into which academic track the pupil shall be placed for the next two years.

There will be three academic tracks, and each of them shall have a slightly different focus. The first track is mainly technical and practical; the second is mainly academic and intellectual; and the third is remedial. Each track will be comprised of elements of socialization, practical skill and cultural knowledge, but the focus will be different (and the course work may be more- or less-rigorous in one track or another.)

Schools shall be segregated by sex, for each sex learns in its own preferred way. Students shall wear identifying uniforms.

We will have ten years' worth of courses of study. With an ideal work rate, a student would enter Year One at age seven or eight, and leave Year 10 at age 18 or 19. However, education shall take as long as necessary. No student shall be required to attend past age 15 except by the wishes of his parents or guardians. Students shall take exit exams each year to determine if they have gained the knowledge necessary to continue. If they have not successfully learned everything taught in that year, they shall repeat the whole year's course of study; recall that we are after a holistic approach to pedagogy.

We shall encourage men to teach boys. It is of utmost importance that men learn from men, for only men can teach boys to become men. One of the failings in the West and especially in multi-racial Western countries is the plague of fatherless boys. This is compounded by the dearth of male teachers for young boys and men. It's critically important that boys learn from men and have male role models and mentors.

Part IV. Academics and Practicum

In each of these, we shall give deference to classic and enduring works of Western thought over those of other traditions and of more recent vint. We shall construct lists of Great Books upon which to build our education on each of these subjects, the value of which shall ensure valuable education in all three facets of school.

The ten academic subjects of study appropriate to a school:

Christian Doctrine and Practice

Composition and Rhetoric

Classics and Poetry

Economics: macro, micro, investing, and personal finance

Etiquette, manners, and social grace

History: ancient, antiquity, medieval and modern, with a focus on the continuity, traditions, accomplishments and culture of our European forebears

Languages: Greek and Latin, then others

Law, Government and Political Science and Practice

Arithmetic, Geometry, Applied Maths, Pure Maths, and Engineering

Physical Science: physics, chemistry and biology

Not every academic subject shall be offered to both sexes. The sexes are different and complimentary and we will strongly encourage people to assume their appropriate and God-given gender roles.

The 16 applied subjects of study appropriate to school:[9]

Animal husbandry and horticulture

Architecture

---

[9] Subject to change and expansion to meet future needs.

Carpentry: home building, cabinetry and joinery and other

Childcare

Classical 2D and 3D art

Digital Arts and Sciences

Farming

Forestry and Land Management

Home economics including cooking, cleaning, home maintenance and first aid

Machine work and smithing

Medicine

Military science and the Christian principles of warfare

Outdoor survival including game hunting

Skilled labor trades

Urban planning and pacification

Military arts, including use of firearms and greater weapons

Again, not every applied subject will be offered to both sexes.

Paper Six. The Nature of Church.

Part I. Preamble.

All people from all places on the Earth, in the present era and on in perpetuity, have been shown the path of Eternal Salvation through Jesus Christ[10]. Additionally, it is self-evident that leading a Christian life gives each person his best chance to be happy and succeed in his aspirations. It is therefore especially incumbent upon us as a Republic to continually renew these teachings and spread the Good News.

Herein we will make no specific theological claims above and beyond the consensus found at Nicaea[11], but rather focus on the structure of the church and its impact on civic life.

---

[10] On may quibble with the "all" here. Let us stipulate to an infinitesimal hyperbole.
[11] And with some broad caveats with respect to Christian vice and virtue inlaid.

Part II. Church Doctrine.

Note that we do not lay out any specific theological arguments or specific dogma here. These proscriptions are broadly laid. Those with greater knowledge and care for the Scriptures shall serve to create the theological infrastructure to support the church we so describe.

While the people as individuals and in their several voluntary associations may decide to do this as their own choice, the republic shall also establish an especial and promoted Christian Church, which we shall call the Second Republican Church or some other suitable name which references our great country. It shall be an explicitly Protestant church, whose tenets include a personal petition to God. We shall say that Almighty God shall have a personal relationship with the faithful rather than requiring intercession from the particular church of our realm. We shall as well hold to the doctrine of *Sola Fide*, or salvation through faith alone.

The Church shall instill in men the several **Ecclesiastical Virtues**, and warn against the predations of the several corresponding **Deadly Sins**. (Christians of our time shall know these.[12])

[12] The Ecclesiastical Virtues are: Chastity, Temperance, Charity, Diligence, Patience, Gratitude, Humility, Economy and Care. The corresponding Sins in the same order are: Lust, Gluttony, Greed, Sloth, Wrath, Envy, Pride, Vainglory and Acedia.

It is incumbent upon the Second Republican Church to assist persons *as persons*, *as a community*, and *as a whole people*, to hold fast to these virtues and avoid these vices; and to actively practice those activities which advance the virtuous causes related to each virtue and stamp out each vice.

Ecclesiastic Virtues

The first Ecclesiastical Virtue is **Chastity. Chastity** is the purity of the body; freedom from all unlawful commerce of sexes. Before marriage, chastity is purity from all commerce of sexes; after marriage, fidelity to the marriage bed.

Its corresponding vice is **Lust. Lust** is concupiscence[13]; carnal appetite; unlawful desire of carnal pleasure. It is also evil propensity; depraved affections and desires.

The Second Ecclesiastical Virtue is **Temperance. Temperance** is moderation; particularly, habitual moderation in with regard to the indulgence of natural appetites and passions. **Temperance** is also calmness, sedateness and moderation of passionate emotions; for thinking and acting under the influence of these emotions is deleterious to a good life[14].

---

[13] Unlawful appetite for sex; sexual deviancy.
[14] Compare to the civic virtue of the same name.

Its corresponding vice is **Gluttony. Gluttony** is the excess of consumption; extravagant indulgence of any kind; and the voracity of appetite.

The Third Ecclesiastical Virtue is **Charity (or Generosity.)** In a general sense, this is love, benevolence, good will; that disposition of heart which inclines men to think favorably of their fellow man, and to do them good. In a theological sense, it includes supreme love to God, and universal good will to men. **Charity** also means liberality to the poor, consisting of private and/or ecclesiastical almsgiving or benefactions, or in gratuitous service to relieve their burdens[15].

Its corresponding vice is **Greed. Greed** is a keenness of appetite in excess of what is needed, or the habitual desire to attain greater wealth or other valuable things regardless of need. **Greed differs from Gluttony** because Greed is an *aspiration*, while Gluttony is an *act*.

The Fourth Ecclesiastical Virtue is **Diligence. Diligence** is the steady application in business of any kind; constant effort to accomplish what is undertaken; exertion of body or mind without unnecessary delay.

---

[15] There is no virtue to state or government relief, for governments have no sentiment of their own. That which is given by government must first be taken from others. Specifically, that which is taken by force is not virtuous, but rather vicious.

Its corresponding vice is **Sloth. Sloth** is disinclination to action or labor; sluggishness; laziness; idleness.

The Fifth Ecclesiastical Virtue is **Patience. Patience** is the ability to suffer afflictions, pain, toil, calamity or other setback or evil with a calm, unruffled temper. It is the endurance to weather adversity. Patience may spring from constitutional fortitude or from Christian submission to God's will[16]. Patience is also the quality of bearing offenses and injuries without anger or revenge.

Its corresponding vice is **Wrath. Wrath** is violent anger, vehement exasperations, indignation expressed, offense taken to excess, or the act of taking justice into one's own hands rather than delegating it to appointed authority.

The Sixth Ecclesiastical Virtue is **Gratitude. Gratitude** is an emotion of the hears, excited by a favor or benefit received; especially God's mercy and His grace. It is a sentiment of goodwill towards a benefactor; thankfulness in all bounties. Gratitude is an agreeable emotional state and a disposition to make sure to recognize and utilize suitable return on the gifts received; not to waste that which has been given. The love of God is the sublimest gratitude.

---

[16] Compare to the civic virtue of Fortitude.

Its corresponding vice is **Envy. Envy** is the feeling of uneasiness, mortification or discontent at the sight of superior excellence. It is longing to take from another that which they have unlawfully or unethically. It is a confession of inferiority to the object of the envy. As all men are created equal before God, it is especially important to remember that no man is inferior to another. **Envy** is also to begrudge, or to withhold maliciously.

The Seventh Ecclesiastical Virtue is **Humility.** In a *theological* sense, **Humility** consists of lowliness of mind; a deep sense of one's own unworthiness in the eyes of God; self-abasement, penitence, and submission to the divine will. In a broad sense, **Humility** is freedom from pride and arrogance. It is a humbleness of mind. It is a modest and realistic sense of one's own worth.

Its corresponding vice is **Pride. Pride** is an excess of self-esteem; weighing one's own value as greater than it is in some specific or in general. It is insolence; it is rude treatment of others[17].

The Eighth Ecclesiastical Virtue is **Economy. Economy** in this sense is a frugal and efficient use of resources, particularly avoiding ostentation and pomp. It extends past money to every resource necessary for a given task or mission. For God has given us our ability as well as the raw materials necessary to create; therefore we

---

[17] There are less-negative definitions of the word which have come into common use, but these are not applicable here.

take it to be sinful to waste any of our ability or raw materials in the process of creation and betterment.

Its corresponding vice is **Vainglory. Vainglory** is vanity excited and expressed by one's own performances or deeds; empty pride; excessive vanity; excessive self-promotion. It is also the miscarriage of the command of those people and things under your command for personal gain. *cf.* A Vainglorious battle is one where a general orders an attack, costing lives and materièl when no such attack is necessary.

The Ninth Ecclesiastical Virtue is **Care. Care** is the thoughtfulness and action necessary to maintain that which is good in oneself or in another; to sustain a good thing or a person; a feeling (rather than an expression) of protectiveness and the action inspired by that feeling.

Its corresponding vice is **Acedia, or (Neglect.) Acedia** is to overlook via carelessness or by design; to allow to fall into disuse or disrepair; to overlook or fail to notice the suffering in others; to disrespect one's own body, mind and spirit, allowing them to deteriorate. It also means to slight or exclude someone rudely from an activity with undue prejudice.

Part III. Church Facilities.

The Church will be a separate entity from the public government. This is to say the Republic shall not be a theocracy. Christian men will be more than welcome to apply their faith to the process of governance. But as it may, it will be incumbent upon the several people, and not through their government, to build houses of worship as they see fit.

Churches and their real holdings shall remain untaxed only as long as the church maintains fidelity to its duties as enumerated above: transmission of moral and religious culture and the facilitation of commune with God. This fidelity shall be judged first by the town or city in which that church is founded, then when necessary by the normal judicial authorities. This judgment shall only be to whether the church has held to its duties; any crimes alleged shall be adjudicated separately.

Paper Seven. On Trades and Professions.

Part I. Preamble.

Each kind of industry shall naturally form a certain relationship with the public based on its nature. We see in diverse places and diverse times across our world that the same patterns persist naturally, prior to any government interference in those industries.

However, governments do interfere with industries to different extents based on both the government and the industry, creating new patterns and relationships. These economic and structural patterns are based partially on the openness, or liberality of the overall economy, and partially as inherent to the business: whether it requires a great deal of skilled labor, a great deal of capital, or neither or both; whether a particular industry's efficiencies of scale result in many competitors, or only one. We shall discuss the kinds of economies and kinds of relationships between the several industries and the public in a future paper. However, there are some general axioms which we can posit now regardless of the types and kinds of relationships in any given economic circumstance.

Part II. Private Property.

Businesses of all sizes may control their own private property. They have an inalienable right to the pursuit of property and the pursuit of wealth created therefrom. That which is not owned by private entities belongs to the whole of the people in common, with some level of government as custodian.

Tax on real holdings is forbidden. Every entity owns his property outright or has established another means to finance it. The government shall not abridge ownership through tax, duty, levy or lien. Tax on ephemeral resource, such as stock and other financial instruments, is exempt from this forbiddance.

The limited liability corporation held in common by several parties being necessary to secure liberty against postmodernism, the right of the people to access free, equal and fair trade shall not be publicly or privately infringed.

Part III. Antitrust.

What is Antitrust? Antitrust is the concept of restraining entities of great capital from distorting or dominating a market at the expense of competition and at the expense of the consumer or public. We shall take great pains to restrain the dominance of any one actor within an industry, and furthermore to restrict the impact of any one industry on the culture as a whole. We have outlined an example of this concept in a prior paper[18].

Part IV. Collective Bargaining.

What is a Union? A Union is an organization of workers formed for the purpose of advancing members' interests with respect to wages, benefits and working conditions.
Unions shall be allowed in businesses which:

- Are privately owned, and
- Receive less than half of their revenue from public sources.

Public (government) unions shall be strictly prohibited.

Union-employee coercion or mandatory membership shall be strictly prohibited.

Furthermore, union organizations shall be under the same Antitrust scrutiny as any other powerful private entity, for the unchecked power of a union may be likewise deleterious to the Republic and its people.

---

[18] Paper Four part II.

Part V. Safety and Oversight.

It shall be incumbent upon industries to keep work environments safe and to provide just compensation for those injured in the course of their work. This policy shall be monitored by some level of government, and enforced *non-punitively* through *just* fines, strictly avoiding *retaliation* or *prosecutorial discretion,* coupled with providing the public with the information necessary to make informed decisions about employment and commerce.

Part VI. Free Association.

As the legal embodiment of a free people, the government shall be forbidden from setting any quota or demographic restriction on those who participate in any business, aside from that which protects children from inappropriate labor.

Paper Eight. On Intransitive Demographics.

Part I. Preamble.

Intransitive demographics are those characteristics of an individual which he cannot change. These include sex, age, intelligence, inherent height, phenotype and ancestry among others.

Hair color and skin color are readily changed; tattoos or other markings can be added or subtracted; a man may become wealthy or become destitute; he may become pious or worldly. Furthermore each kind of person has a kind of task which he is most likely suitable. None of these qualities are intransitive, and each can be shaped somewhat by the culture.

Part II. Affect.

Cultural harmony being better than multicultural discord, we shall encourage in all matters a unified culture and an aspiration to the Heroic ideal. Some will take to this better than others. In the case of phenotype, it is broadly an indicator of culture and intelligence; in the case of sex, it is broadly an indicator of level of temperance and reason among other qualities.

Therefore at a very basic level; as a foundation of the Republic, we must keep the people whole in blood and in culture. With these two unifying characteristics intact, there is scarcely a set of laws which will result in ruin. But without these, no set of laws will suffice to manage a free people.

When it comes to the two sexes, there are roles in society better played by men and others better suited to women. These are not absolutes, but rather useful generalizations. Therefore, as we have seen in the section on Schools and on Families, we shall in all matters respect the difference between the sexes rather than force an un-natural egalitarianism upon them. This too promotes cultural harmony, for it provides for each sex to serve in the role for which Nature has better prepared it.

Paper Nine. States, Regimes, and Governments.

Part I. Preamble.

Why did we spend so much time on things other than the government?

States are not the only kinds of polities men have enacted over time, but they are the most efficient and stable that we know about now. Nearly all the world is controlled by one state or another; those places which are not are unsuitable or unattractive for conquest and management.

But states are not the same thing as governments. There are three components which the layman will sometimes conflate: States, Regimes, and Governments.

Part II. Definitions.

What is a State? A State, as we have said, is **a** legal entity that maintains a defined territory and maintains a monopoly on the lawful use of deadly force within that territory. Over and above that there are some other features that some states have, but these are the bare minimum requirements for an entity to be called a state.

What is a Regime? States have within them Regimes. A Regime is the set of rules and norms of that state's politics, upon which their government is based. The Roman Empire's Regime was that of one or a small number of Emperors, advised by a Senate, overseeing a large military dictatorship. The City-States of Greece had regimes usually based upon direct democracy with suffrage granted to a small electorate. As we write, The Vatican has the only world regime with an elected absolute monarch – although the College of Cardinals who so elect him is very small indeed.

Regimes are less permanent than States. Any given state may have a number of various regimes. For instance, France has gone through numerous stages of Monarchy and Republic, some turning over in only a few years. But whether France has one or the other, it is still France. On the other hand, the United States had the same regime (the First Constitution) for 232 years before becoming an illiberal regime[19]. San Marino has survived under one regime for over 1600 years.

What is a Government? Still less permanent are **Governments**. Governments are the particular people and institutions in place in a given iteration of a regime. The layman may use these words interchangeably. In fact, the idea of "the government falling" may send alarm through those people who consider "the government" to be the same as "the regime" as well as "the state." But any government is temporal. Presidents are elected and then leave office; even a king must die someday.

Consider Regime as the Regime the machine of state, and the Government its operators.

What is Policy? Policy is the specific plan a particular government enacts, based on laws, regulations, marketing and coercion. A minimum wage is an example of a policy, as is military adventurism. There are an arbitrarily large number of Policy choices.

What is Politics? Politics is the struggle in any group for power that will give one or more persons the ability to make decisions for the larger group. This can happen within a family just as much as in a state or even the world.

When it comes to public politics, it is the struggle for the power to

---

[19] The type of which is still unclear at the time of this writing.

make decisions on behalf of a subset or the whole of the people. Or we can think of it as the hiring process for that skilled labor, or even the choice of which machinery to use in the first place.

Part III. Political Concerns.

Unified Culture

As politics is the struggle for power to make decisions for a group, it follows that the more-unified the group, the closer the distinctions between the several leaders, and the smaller the window of policy choices necessary to satisfy the stakeholders. While this smaller range of choices will not make the process less acrimonious[20], it will lead to choices which are more amenable to the out-groups within the polity. That is, the choices that are made will be closer to the cultural norm than those that might be made in a multicultural state.

Moral Culture

Ideals have little place in practical politics, and this is why: the decisions necessary to attain and maintain political power will inevitably conflict with the moral and ethical aspirations of politicians. Those politicians who maintain their ideals above their quest for power will therefore inevitably be conquered by those

---

[20] Consider Dr. Seuss' *Butter Battle Book*, &c.

willing to put the pursuit of power above their ideals.

Therefore in order to regulate our politics to a great degree and to reward virtue in the pursuit of political power, it is of utmost importance that we have a moral and ethical people; and that the path to power is very closely guided by those people. It is for this reason among others that we have defined our people, our citizens, and our cultural institutions prior to defining any kind of Regime.

Paper Ten. On Suffrage and Franchise.

Part I. Preamble.

Suffrage is the domain of those diligent men, who head households, and is practiced on behalf of the Family. Let us now define this suffrage and explain why it should be as expansive as it is.

Part II. Definitions.

Recall our definition of a **Citizen**. In Part:

A Citizen is a Person whose Parents are both citizens, or a Person who has gone through a stringent legal test of cultural compatibility and economic value to the Republic and has subsequently been naturalized and granted permanent citizenship. The responsibilities and benefits of Citizenship shall be defined elsewhere and by statute as required. A Citizen will owe his national allegiance to the Republic and strive to advance her power relative to other countries; and the Republic shall in all events put the welfare of a Citizen above that of any other Person.

And recall our definition of **Family**:

A Family is a number of people larger than one, related primarily through marriage or blood, that live together more or less permanently.

While God has endowed each Person with the inalienable rights of life, liberty and the pursuit of wealth among many other things, the indivisible unit of the Republic is the Family. Families sustain and propagate the Republic; an individual cannot do it alone.

What is Suffrage? Suffrage is a voice, a vote, a prayer, a publicly-spoken aspiration. It is the rightful voice of the rightful citizen to correctly direct the Regime and its Government. Because of the sustaining power of the family, it is morally correct for the People to vest in that single institution the responsibility of Suffrage.

What is Franchise? Franchise is a particular privilege or right granted by the Sovereign to an individual or to a number of persons; as the right to be a body corporate with perpetual succession; the right to hold accountable the regime on its actions and behavior; and a right that belongs to citizens only and not to any or all aliens.

Part III. Franchise.

Responsibility and Right

Almost universally, our discourse today considers voting only as a right. But rather than thinking of it this way, let's consider that voting is the most direct way for the average voter to direct the ship of state. And when the ship of state hits the rocks, it will be laid upon the backs of those voters to bear the cost to right it, whether that be financial or something far worse.

Therefore voting is a grave responsibility. Consider this aspect of voting, what could go very wrong on a very large scale, before considering the value of it as a right. When we consider voting in this light, it is something not to be sought out lightly, but rather a mantle to take up on behalf of man's political creation.

In this paper we shall show that it is morally and functionally correct to keep the voting population much smaller than it has been traditionally in those failed states of our origins.

On The Importance of Family

Let us focus on the phrase: *Body corporate with perpetual succession.*

No individual, on his own, no matter how successful he may be, shall be the recipient of Suffrage, for he has not demonstrated Franchise. A man without a family cannot be trusted fully with a voice on the future of the Republic for he himself has no future.

Furthermore, to grant suffrage to more than one member of a family is to pit Father against Son, and Husband against Wife. Since a family is more important than a State, being the building block of the Nation, suffrage shall be held as subordinate to familial tranquility. Therefore in the interest of domestic tranquility, the responsibility of voting shall be limited to only one vote per family.

To the ear of a modern liberal listener of our contemporary *zeitgeist*, this may seem to favor the old over the young, the man over the woman and the smaller family over large ones. However, this is the bias of the listener and not of the system of suffrage. Those who have been reared in the postmodernist, post-Western traditions of the 20th and 21st centuries put the individual at the center of man's existence. Therefore "stripping" the power of any one individual and handing it over to another will seem strange and unfair.

However, prior to the 20th century, people of the West instinctively understood that there was a hierarchy to the world and would be suspicious of any system of egalitarianism or "fairness" in the modern sense. To the historical man, fairness was a near-synonym to justice: it consisted of giving each person what he has earned.

The modern man will consider fairness in a different context: equality of outcomes.

Having judged this postmodern time as lacking and moreover destructive of personal happiness and cultural cohesion, we now make the choice to return to a hierarchical paradigm where those men who lead families will decide (with appropriate input) how to direct the Nation, State, Regime and Government, regardless of the size of family with which God and fortune have blessed them.

On the Ethical Quandary of Self-Dealing

Civilian governmental employees of any kind, and those workers in firms which receive half or more of their compensation from the Government as customer, shall forego suffrage because it is a conflict of interest. For they are, in essence, voting money from the Treasury directly into their own purse; betraying the State to serve themselves.

Therefore these men and their families will recuse themselves from voting or contributing to political causes for as long as these conditions hold true. Even if there is no impropriety, it is the appearance of impropriety that is unethical. Therefore consider that these men still hold Franchise, but will not be allowed to exercise it during the terms of these arrangements.

On Women and Voting

Women by their Nature are not suited to blind and faithful governance over a large body of people. While men are, on average, consumed by *acquisition,* women are, on average, consumed by *distribution.* A man shall find it good to acquire as much as he can, while a woman shall find it good to distribute that bounty equally among several petitioners.

We have seen over time that immutable human nature produces the same patterns over and over. About 4 men in 10 are the fathers to each new generation; about 8 women in 10 are the mothers to the same. This is because in order for a man to pass on his family line, he must acquire wealth and fame in order to show his fitness to father children. On the other hand, women are best served by being agreeable within their sisterhood, so as to avoid being cast out, unavailable for these few exceptional men.

Prolific fathers must be *exceptional*; prolific mothers must be *agreeable.* Therefore God and Nature have conspired to make women agreeable.

Women are made to be communal, the anchor to their tribe. One of the strongest bonds between a people is their shared beliefs. These form the basis of Culture. When an authority emplaces an idea within the tribe, be it good or bad, women will most readily and pleasingly adopt the idea. They are in this way more malleable and subject to control.

And conversely, the woman who shall reject this control shall be pilloried and shunned by her sisters, painted as a poor prospect for mothering.

It is hard for a woman to break conditioning, to strike out from her sisters; to think for herself and make reasoned decisions.

It is this natural submission to the ideas of the group, natural affinity for distribution above acquisition, and both cultural and inherent difficulty with directed and energetically-independent thought that makes women unsuitable for franchise. Therefore women shall be denied suffrage based on their feminine nature.

On Single Men Voting

God and Nature have also shown us that the passions of youthful men can prevent their cooler heads from prevailing; it also takes time to master wisdom. Therefore at the minimum, a man must attain the age of 21 before he receives the Franchise.

Man without land, without a home, may have great love for his country; but he has no financial stake in the present. Therefore men who do not wholly or partly own their own home shall not receive the franchise; and they will only vote in the polity wherein they primarily domicile.

Part IV. Conclusion.

Now we have limited the Franchise thusly:

- One vote per family, for families sustain the State; and men without families have no future;
- Excepting those in civil service due to potential and obvious conflict of interest;
- Excepting women for their feminine nature is unsuitable for governance;
- Excepting very young men for their wild passions and lack of wisdom; and
- Excepting men without land, for they have no stake in the present.

Laying the burden of Suffrage upon the shoulders of so many in our Republic shall lighten that burden for each individual man. But increasing the franchise further than this shall immediately give a foothold for pernicious ruin.

Paper Eleven. On the Several Forms of Government and Elections.

Part I. Preamble.

Thus far, we have talked in very general terms about the republic. We have not, however, given mention to types of regime enacted in states in various times and places. Let us now define these other forms of government to give better perspective to that which is good about the Republic and that which a republic might lack.

Part II. Definitions of Types of Regime.

A Monarchy is a Regime in which the power of sovereignty is vested in the hands of a single person. Usually this state is called an empire, or a kingdom or principality, regardless of the monarch's sex.

The same name, or the name **Constitutional Monarchy,** is often given to a state where the Regime has a sovereign ruler also guided by a written constitution limiting his powers and delegating some of those powers to some groups of Citizens.

A Monarchy made up of many smaller indivisible states is called an **Empire**. Each part of an empire will have its own culture, customs and laws but they will fall under the control of the greater whole[21].

A Tyranny is an illiberal regime where sovereignty is vested in one man or a small group of men, such as the generals of a state's armed forces. The sovereign may exercise arbitrary or despotic powers not bound by rigorous law or justice or not for the purpose of governance. The people of the state have little if any control over the government.

One kind of tyranny is the **Theocracy,** wherein secular and ecclesiastical power are held by the same person or people. Although rare today, there are examples of Theo-Monarchy as well.

Another kind of tyranny is the **Illiberal Democracy**, wherein the rulers wear the trappings of a republic such as elections and separation of powers, but true power is not vested in the whole of the people. These devices are meant for show and stripped of any meaning.

---

[21] Certainly there are empires which are not monarchies, but the historical precedent tends in that direction.

An Oligarchy is government by unelected elite, usually one derived from great wealth. An Oligarchy is often a kind of Illiberal Democracy, presenting the façade of a Republic to the world. Many oligarchies will abuse their power in subtle ways in order to maintain plausible deniability for their number, who are, theoretically, bound by the laws of the state.

A Democracy is government by the whole of the people; a form of government in which sovereignty is vested in the people collectively, or in which the people exercise the powers of legislation. The Democracy has no separation of powers or provision to check the power of brute-force decision making. It is unstable and chaotic, for any given law or custom may be changed without warning. Democracies tend to evolve into other kinds of governments because of the inherently unstable nature of the regime.

A Republic is an indivisible nation, within which the supreme authority, or sovereignty, rests within the entirety of the citizenry rather than in a single individual, its military, some guild or religious group, or some external authority entirely. In a Republic, some significant portion of the whole of the people express the general will through electing men to whom they delegate their authority to rule. Therefore Republics, among all these governments, are the one form which affords true agency to the great body of its citizens.

Part III. Regimes and Elections.

An Election is the act of choosing from more than one choice. In the case of politics, it means to choose an office of employment in the government. Those who are elected to government in this matter are granted license by those who choose him to wield some of the authority vested in the electorate.

In a Democracy, there is no election; the power of sovereignty inherent to the people is translated by vote directly into the deadly force of the government to enact its will.

In a Republic or Constitutional Monarchy, elections are held as they are defined in a Constitution.

Delegates serve for fixed periods and fill fixed roles as defined in a Constitution.

Illiberal Democracies and Oligarchies will usually hold elections, but these are part of the illusion of general sovereignty rather than a true exercise of such power. The choices presented may be unusually narrow; the elections may be fraught with corruption; courts may be established to neuter or overturn decisions deemed impermissible by the rulers.

Therefore the act of electing itself is a fundamental element to a Republic; and conversely, Republics are the most effective regime in protecting the liberty and sovereignty of the people. Elections are central to protecting those rights endowed in us by God, and therefore there is an element of the sacred within the institution. And therefore it is of supreme importance for a people to have free and fair elections, every time, to the best of their ability.

Part IV. Free and Fair Elections.

Since a republic's legitimacy rests upon doing the will of the people as expressed in the main at the ballot box, we shall ensure accurate accounting of votes, accurate reporting of votes, public availability of the process and specific evidence of same, and the privacy of any individual's secret ballot.

Corruption in elections being the great enemy of liberty and national legitimacy, we shall establish specific and well-tested means for protecting election and vote integrity and for validating the results of such elections.

Furthermore we shall reserve the greatest punishments for those who adulterate our highest of civic duties: that of managing our bounty for Posterity through the act of voting.

The People generally must know and shall know that the vote is counted accurately. He who casts a vote must know that his vote is tallied correctly. And those men from around the World must know that our Government and Regime are legitimate, and not subject to arbitrary change from the outside. Therefore the People shall have open access to this process for the purpose of verification and inquest into any irregularities which may appear.

Just as important as transparency in the counting and oversight of the result is the secrecy of the ballot. While men may choose to present ideas to one another in public, each man's choice is a sacred and secret Covenant between himself and the entirety of the Sovereign; only he and no other party may choose to make that decision public.

Secrecy is also necessary to keep peace when one man may strongly disagree with another, or when a group of men may put another under duress to sway his vote.

Paper Twelve. Secure Elections.

Part I. Preamble.

Free and secure elections form the foundation of any representational regime and subsequent government. Without this fundamental feature, the regime is illiberal and by its own definition, illegitimate.

No set of laws can completely ensure free and fair elections because people are imperfectable. However, with strong guidance from our civic virtues coupled with the following rules, statutes shall be constructed to mitigate any fraud committed against the Republic in the process of these, the most sacred of civic events.

Furthermore, the *appearance* of impropriety and the *appearance* of fraud shall shake the confidence and unity of the people. Should there be significant uncertainty or good evidence of vote fraud, whether it has actually occurred or not, some portion of the people shall no longer trust in the regime. A regime without the trust of the people is a regime without consent. Therefore even the appearance of fraud puts into question the regime's legitimacy.

Part II. Rules. [22]

1. All voting processes other than those necessary to preserve the secret ballot shall be open and available for direct observation with no minimum distance requirement, and for the audit by agents of the candidates and their political parties, as well as interested third parties.

2. All official documents and work product related to the election shall have a secure chain of custody at all times. Election officials shall be accompanied by observers when accessing any election materials. Records of the chain of custody shall be complete and available for audit.

3. All votes, regardless of voting method, shall be held to the same standard.

4. Voters shall be only qualified Citizens who can demonstrate, through official documents, their legal right to vote. These documents shall include government-issued photo ID, proof of primary residency, and proof of ownership of same in the form of government records or bank records.

5. As a condition for receiving a ballot, each person shall record his name in a Poll Book.

---

[22] *Adapted from the Kootenai County, Idaho, US, GOP Citizens Committee for Election Integrity* https://www.kootenaigop.org/blog/2021/1/8/minimum-standard-for-fair-and-honest-elections

6. Ballots shall have a physical form which allows voting choices to be examined by the naked eye and easily recognized by a layman.

7. Ballots shall have features to avoid counterfeiting, as with currency or prescription pads.

8. An auditable system for tracking the status of all ballots shall be implemented and maintained by the National Government. The total number of printed ballots shall be equal to the sum of cast ballots, spoiled ballots and uncast ballots.

9. Ballot tabulation shall be conducted by at least two independent and unrelated systems. These systems shall not be connected to the Internet or to one another. The difference in totals between the two systems shall be less than one half the margin of victory or 0.1%, whichever is the smaller sum. Tabulating machines shall only tabulate, and not modify ballots in any way.

10. Before results may be certified, the ballot counts shall be reconciled with voter records.

11. Voter rolls shall be purged of unqualified Citizens 180 days before any election, except for snap elections for the House of Delegates. Voter Rolls shall be compared against official government records to identify persons, living or dead, who have left the locality or have lost their right to vote.

12. Laws which pertain to elections shall not be changed for 180 days prior to a general election and shall not be changed prior to a spontaneous (snap) election.

13. All election records shall be preserved and maintained for a minimum of five years.

14. No provisional ballots shall be issued.

Appendix I: Civic Virtues and Ecclesiastic Virtues

Part I. Preamble.

We have defined six Civic Virtues and their corresponding Vices in Paper Two. In Paper Three, we have named the nine Ecclesiastic Virtues and their corresponding Sins, but we have not defined them. For ease of reference, the fifteen pairs are presented here.

Part II. Civic Virtues.

A Hero, or Complete Citizen, has six primary virtues. They must be collected in this specific order, for each is built upon the foundation of the previous ones, like a pyramid.

Virtue One is to keep **Truth at the center of the mind**. This means that a man must always seek to know things as they are rather than how he wishes them to be. A man with truth at the center of his mind will prefer an abhorrent truth to a comforting lie.

Its corresponding Vice is **Narrativism**, which means that a man must first construct a worldview which pleases him, and then fit the facts to this narrative.

Virtue Two is to practice **Right Reason**. This means that a man must believe that there is one true description of reality, and that he must apply his senses and intellect to discern what it is.

Its corresponding Vice is **Postmodernism**, which states there is no one correct frame of reference and that each opinion on reality is equally valid. Of all the Vices, this is the most poisonous to the Republic and must be fought against trenchantly at every Time and in every Place.

Virtue Three is **Prudence**. Prudence demands **caution of deliberation** on the most suitable means to accomplish valuable purposes, and the exercise of sagacity in discerning and selecting them. It differs from wisdom in that Prudence is more cautious and less spontaneous. Inalienable to Prudence is the saying, "First Do No Harm." Also inalienable is preparing for things which may go wrong (or go right) according to the application of the first two Virtues.

Its corresponding Vice is **Carelessness**. The misapplication of spontaneity results in negligence and harm. When a man is not instilled with discipline and responsibility he is prone to carelessness.

Virtue Four is **Justice**. Justice consists of giving every man his due. It pertains to men dealing with other men or to groups. In the case of the legal system of the Republic, it consists of the whole body of

Citizens, at times of official legal conflict, bestowing upon each man what he is due.

Its corresponding Vice is **Fiat**, wherein a subject gives to an object what the subject desires to give, regardless of what the object deserves. While God has the power of Fiat, no man nor body of men shall practice it, for they are limited and have not the ability to marry Fiat to Justice. In God there are no irreconcilable contradictions, but this is not true for Men in this World.

Virtue Five is **Fortitude**. Fortitude is the ability to weather the physical, intellectual, emotional and moral strain of existence and to persevere in the face of adversity.

Its corresponding Vice is **Victimhood**, wherein a man attempts to achieve social, moral or other superiority over others by claiming prior injury at some other hand.

Virtue Six is **Temperance, which is the practice of moderation**; particularly habitual moderation in the indulgence of the several natural appetites and passions. Temperance also refers to moderation in the times and places where Justice shall be offered, for a man must know where to act and where to pause his actions in delivering outcome.

Its corresponding Vice is **Abandon**, wherein a man allows himself to fall to a deadly sin when he could otherwise prevent it.

A man who achieves mastery of these six Virtues shall be considered to have achieved the pinnacle of citizenship. Therefore we shall construct our culture to transmit and lionize these virtues and to defend against their corresponding vices in all matters.

Part III. Ecclesiastic Virtues.

The first Ecclesiastical Virtue is **Chastity. Chastity** is the purity of the body; freedom from all unlawful commerce of sexes. Before marriage, chastity is purity from all commerce of sexes; after marriage, fidelity to the marriage bed.

Its corresponding vice is **Lust. Lust** is concupiscence[23]; carnal appetite; unlawful desire of carnal pleasure. It is also evil propensity; depraved affections and desires.

The Second Ecclesiastical Virtue is **Temperance. Temperance** is moderation; particularly, habitual moderation in with regard to the indulgence of natural appetites and passions. **Temperance** is also calmness, sedateness and moderation of passionate emotions; for thinking and acting under the influence of these emotions is deleterious to a good life[24].

---

[23] Unlawful appetite for sex; sexual deviancy.

[24] Compare to the civic virtue of the same name.

Its corresponding vice is **Gluttony. Gluttony** is the excess of consumption; extravagant indulgence of any kind; and the voracity of appetite.

The Third Ecclesiastical Virtue is **Charity (or Generosity.)** In a general sense, this is love, benevolence, good will; that disposition of heart which inclines men to think favorably of their fellow man, and to do them good. In a theological sense, it includes supreme love to God, and universal good will to men. **Charity** also means liberality to the poor, consisting of private and/or ecclesiastical almsgiving or benefactions, or in gratuitous service to relieve their burdens[25].

Its corresponding vice is **Greed. Greed** is a keenness of appetite in excess of what is needed, or the habitual desire to attain greater wealth or other valuable things regardless of need. **Greed differs from Gluttony** because Greed is an *aspiration*, while Gluttony is an *act*.

The Fourth Ecclesiastical Virtue is **Diligence. Diligence** is the steady application in business of any kind; constant effort to accomplish what is undertaken; exertion of body or mind without unnecessary delay.

---

[25] There is no virtue to state or government relief, for governments have no sentiment of their own; and that which is given by government must first be taken from others. Specifically, that which is taken by force is not virtuous, but rather vicious.

Its corresponding vice is **Sloth. Sloth** is disinclination to action or labor; sluggishness; laziness; idleness.

The Fifth Ecclesiastical Virtue is **Patience. Patience** is the ability to suffer afflictions, pain, toil, calamity or other setback or evil with a calm, unruffled temper. It is the endurance to weather adversity. Patience may spring from constitutional fortitude or from Christian submission to God's will[26. Patience is also the quality of bearing offenses and injuries without anger or revenge.

Its corresponding vice is **Wrath. Wrath** is violent anger, vehement exasperations, indignation expressed, offense taken to excess, or the act of taking justice into one's own hands rather than delegating it to appointed authority.

The Sixth Ecclesiastical Virtue is **Gratitude. Gratitude** is an emotion of the hears, excited by a favor or benefit received; especially God's mercy and His grace. It is a sentiment of goodwill towards a benefactor; thankfulness in all bounties. Gratitude is an agreeable emotional state and a disposition to make sure to recognize and utilize suitable return on the gifts received; not to waste that which has been given. The love of God is the sublimest gratitude.

---

26 Compare to the civic virtue of Fortitude.

Its corresponding vice is **Envy. Envy** is the feeling of uneasiness, mortification or discontent at the sight of superior excellence. It is longing to take from another that which they have unlawfully or unethically. It is a confession of inferiority to the object of the envy. As all men are created equal before God, it is especially important to remember that no man is inferior to another. **Envy** is also to begrudge, or to withhold maliciously.

The Seventh Ecclesiastical Virtue is **Humility.** In a theological sense, **Humility** consists of lowliness of mind; a deep sense of one's own unworthiness in the eyes of God; self-abasement, penitence, and submission to the divine will. In a broad sense, **Humility** is freedom from pride and arrogance. It is a humbleness of mind. It is a modest and realistic sense of one's own worth.

Its corresponding vice is **Pride. Pride** is an excess of self-esteem; weighing one's own value as greater than it is in some specific or in general. It is insolence; it is rude treatment of others[27].

The Eighth Ecclesiastical Virtue is **Economy. Economy** in this sense is a frugal and efficient use of resources, particularly avoiding ostentation and pomp. It extends past money to every resource necessary for a given task or mission. For God has given us our ability as well as the raw materials necessary to create; therefore we

---

[27] There are less negative definitions of the word which have come into common use but are not applicable here.

take it to be sinful to waste any of our ability or raw materials in the process of creation and betterment.

Its corresponding vice is **Vainglory. Vainglory** is vanity excited and expressed by one's own performances or deeds; empty pride; excessive vanity; excessive self-promotion. It is also the miscarriage of the command of those people and things under your command for personal gain. *cf.* A Vainglorious battle is one where a general orders an attack, costing lives and materièl when no such attack is necessary.

The Ninth Ecclesiastical Virtue is **Care. Care** is the thoughtfulness and action necessary to maintain that which is good in oneself or in another; to sustain a good thing or a person; a feeling (rather than an expression) of protectiveness and the action inspired by that feeling.

Its corresponding vice is **Acedia, or (Neglect.) Acedia** is to overlook via carelessness or by design; to allow to fall into disuse or disrepair; to overlook or fail to notice the suffering in others; to disrespect one's own body, mind and spirit, allowing them to deteriorate. It also means to slight or exclude someone rudely from an activity with undue prejudice.

Appendix II: The Declaration of Liberty

Now we know with certainty about these many violations of the law, and of the public trust around our franchise and our vote; And we have confirmation, unassailable, that this, the one election subject to the pinnacle of scrutiny, can be so be rigged; And we have seen elected officers accede their duty to enforce the law, abetting fraud and thievery; Then we can say that it is possible that any lesser public vote has been so rigged.

And if it's given now that any public vote can be so rigged, we can no longer hold in good fidelity that any public vote has *not* been rigged.

We live as sovereigns of a state; we have endorsed our old regime, defined by founding documents and codified within a written Constitution, which takes its basis for legitimate transaction as the consent of the governed.

Over time, by custom and convention, that consent is given in two forms:

The first is at the voting booth. We vote for several Officers who shall direct the government on our behalf. As we have now seen, this route to give consent has been blocked off.

The second is direct petition of those Officers and of their Agents, by presenting to them, peaceably, our grievances. As we now see, that myriad who have presented grievances unpleasant to the ruling classes' ears are branded dissidents or worse, to be eliminated, rather than be at our liberty to chastise our own government.

Therefore, there is no hint of the consent of the governed; and therefore, by the regime's own definition, they have abdicated their legitimacy.

This is true if we affirm the revocation or do not: the government, in total, and possessing knowledge of their actions and good agency, under this constitutional regime and in this country, have made the decision to rescind their consent to govern us.
We have long seen abuses from our old regime upon the traditional and long-standing People of our nation. These abuses have escalated in magnitude and in number for four generations of Men, and in this Time, become, finally, unforgivable insults against us all.

We have seen the servants in our Government sell out their services to agents of those foreign powers and unpatriotic firms. These officers grow wealthy on ill-gotten gain, their service rightly owed to their constituents or to the whole of the Republic;

We have seen our venal tyrants sell the Bounty of our lands to
foreign countries for their personal gain: the farmlands, the grazing
lands, the minerals and ground fuels, which God has rightly placed
beneath us, on land belonging to us all;

We have seen our generals and our politicians conspire to
perpetuate wars of choice, robbing us of our treasure and our sons;

We have been assaulted and insulted in every possible Manner and
at every possible Time by an unending flood of mass media. It is a
continual blood libel against our traditions and even our lives;

We have seen our rulers export our Trades and Crafts to places
overseas, in the name of cheap labor and greater profits; and
likewise import vast populations to take those jobs which remain,
through un-natural competition, while eating out our assets
through the use of our public institutions;

We have long watched the maltreatment, by neglect or apathy at the
best of times, and outright purpose at the worst, of our Ports and
Borders, allowing entry to any number of Aliens, and encouraging
their invasion with the promise of our wealth;

We have been shut out from the Town Square and been silenced in
the great exchange of ideas, for those ideas of liberty and self-
government run counter to the comfort of ruling classes;

We have seen in the financial sector Government side with the wealthy few as they rig the markets against us; the rich stealing from the poor.

We have witnessed time and again illiberal and unequal application of the law for the personal and political gain of our infidelitous rulers and their masters here and abroad;

And we have felt the cold hand of government at our throat as our suffrage and franchise have been snuffed altogether through massive fraud.

Therefore, due in part to each of these abuses, the sacred compact between the Sovereign people and the Government finally has been severed.

We shall no longer be vassals to a state which has abdicated its responsibilities to us and usurped our Sovereignty.

We abhor tyranny and are suspicious of authority; and our suspicion has been given due now by their tyranny.

We demand a clean break from those venal and obtuse tyrants who have gone before.

As we are a primarily Protestant and thoroughly Christian people;
As we have been persecuted religiously;

As we have been persecuted culturally;

As we have been persecuted as a race of Men;

And as our rulers have silenced our rightful voices through means illegal, unethical and immoral;

When law is unjust and government illegitimate, it is an affront to dignity and to God for good men to abide it. Since law is unjust and the government now illegitimate, we shall not abide it.

We hereby take our liberty from our former countries,

And establish a New Nation, indivisible, tempered by the hand of Free Men, in the Cleansing Fire of God, here upon His sacred Globe. We bequeath this nation to our families and our progeny down through the mists trod only by those future men God finds shall suit His Firmament.

And in reply to each of your grave insults here against our people and against our ancient and significant traditions, we now bequeath to you the one thing you have longed for:

We the Undersigned, leave you to your Realm, our former masters, and bequeath to you our chains.

Let us so declare: We shall now, and forevermore, be free.

Appendix III: The Oath of Citizenship

To be recited before all public gatherings.

As I pursue and practice good Citizenship of the Second Republic, long may it stand;

I pledge to keep **Truth** at the center of my mind
And to avoid in all things **Narrativism**;

I pledge to practice **Right Reason**
And to avoid in all things **Postmodernism**;

I pledge to practice **Prudence**
And to avoid in all things **Carelessness**;

I pledge to be more **Just**
And avoid in all things **Fiat**;

I pledge to gain greater **Fortitude**
And avoid in all things **Victimhood.**

For these are the **Virtues** of Citizens
And the **Vices** of our enemies;
So help me God, Amen.

Appendix IV: The Constitution of the Second Republic

Preamble

The people being Sovereign, and lending their power to the State in times of Consent, do establish this Paper to define the Regime under which our Government shall henceforth be constituted. Furthermore, any law not warranted by this Paper is a bare-faced usurpation, and so we do admonish Men of Posterity to read this document with the intent we emplace within it, with our words as they are used at the time of our Ratification.

This is the Constitution of the Second Republic.

Article I. The Legislature.

Part I. Definitions.

1. All national legislative powers herein granted shall be vested in a Legislature of the Second Republic, which shall consist of a House of Delegates and a Senate. No member of the Executive or Judicial branch shall re-write laws, but may suggest changes and Amendments at the appropriate times.

2. All national legislation shall occur within this body. Local governments shall have power to legislate for their own polities[28].

3. All laws shall expire on the last day of the tenth year of their ratification. Should the legislatures wish to continue a law beyond this date, they must ratify it again during the tenth year[29].

4. No Legislator may serve simultaneously in any other office or capacity within any level of government or as a Lobbyist[30].

5. Each Legislator must divest himself of all Estate, real or temporary, save personal effects, prior to the first day entering office. Such wealth shall be held in a blind trust for the duration of his service. No Delegate may receive compensation from the Treasury greater than the average annual national wage. Furthermore, no Delegate shall have a net worth of greater than 120% of that with which he entered office, the excess to be forfeited to the Treasury upon the last day of each year[31].

6. As this is a Christian nation, each Legislative Delegate shall be a Christian man in practice as well as name.

7. No Legislator may voluntarily resign his position, but may decline to stand for re-election. Should a Legislator require a voluntary resignation, he shall instead be appointed Constable of

---

[28] National legislative supremacy clause.
[29] Sunset clause.
[30] Double-dip clause.
[31] Self-dealing clause.

the Chambers and serve in that role for the remainder of his term and at the same compensation as before.

8. During this time of service as a Constable, he may hold no other position in or out of Government[32].

9. Each Term begins on 7 January or on the day subsequent to the formation of the current Government (less Sundays.) The Legislative Term ends on 17 December. The Legislative Term begins and ends within one calendar year, regardless of any election or other event; this shall not be confused with a Legislator's term in office, which can be of divers lengths.

Each House must meet for at least 30 days per Term and give recess for at least 30 consecutive days each year. Otherwise it must have the permission of the President to adjourn. Each House may have their session and recess at a time it chooses for itself, and requests for adjournment may be submitted separately[33].

The Houses shall not meet on Sundays[34].

10. No Legislator may be held from his duties in his House except for reason of dire infirmity or felony conduct. No Legislator shall be legally sanctioned for his speech or debate within the Chambers[35].

---

[32] Resignation clause, to prevent Legislators from moving from one government job to another during their term, or becoming a lobbyist.

[33] Definition of a term.

[34] Sunday exemption.

[35] Legislative liberty clause.

Part II. The House of Delegates

1. The House of Delegates shall be composed of House Members chosen every fifth year by the citizens of the several districts. Each Delegate shall represent no fewer than 3,500 Citizens and no more than 350,000 Citizens. Delegates must be male Citizens who have reached the age of twenty-five and have lived domestically for the prior five years or longer[36].

2. Districts formed for this representation shall have equal populations. They shall be contiguous and contain no enclaves. They shall be designed by algorithm each tenth year. This algorithm shall be chosen by the Government ten years prior to its enactment except for the first districting. This algorithm shall not take into account any demographic information or information based on Citizens' voluntary associations[37].

3. Populations to be considered shall be based upon a decennial census. The first such census shall be conducted within one calendar year of Ratification; thereafter, redistricting shall occur immediately; thereafter, there shall be an election in each district within 30 days[38].

4. Noncitizens shall receive no representation in number or by Petition[39].

---

[36] Definition of Delegates and their requirements for holding office.
[37] Description of Legislative districts.
[38] Orders a census.
[39] Alien exclusion rule.

5. Each Delegate shall have his primary residence within the borders of his District, and make convenient accommodations to meet with his constituents there regularly throughout the year[40].

6. Delegate seat vacancies which happen between elections shall result in a seat remaining unfilled until the following election[41].

7. Once representatives are chosen, they shall have six days (less Sundays) to form a majority Government. At the end of this period, a Government is formed. If one political party has a simple majority, it may unilaterally and immediately form the Government.

If no single party has a simple majority, each party may attempt to form a coalition between two of more parties to reach majority. But in every case, only the largest majority party has the final say on which other parties or nonparty Delegates shall join in the majority[42].

8. The Delegates not in the Majority are not part of Government, but instead the Shadow Government, which has the power to advise the Government in writing and by speech and debate within the chamber[43].

9. If no majority Government is formed within this period, another Election shall occur in 25 days plus Sundays after the date of such dilemma[44].

---

[40] Residency requirement; local meeting rule.
[41] Delegate vacancy rule.
[42] Formation of Government rule.
[43] Shadow Government rule.

10. Upon the formation of the Government, it shall choose from among its body a Majority Leader to head it. This Leader shall choose from the Government four deputies: A Home Secretary, a Foreign Secretary, a Treasury Secretary and an Attorney General[45].

11. The Majority Leader shall serve as head of Government and its Chief Executive[46].

12. The Home Secretary shall administer to the lands and infrastructure within the Republic and have sole authority to submit legislation to establish and strike such Departments as he deems necessary for these purposes.

13. The Foreign Secretary shall provide, at his sole discretion, a corps of diplomats and support staff for the President's use in representation of the Republic to the world. The Chief Administrator of this corps shall be chosen by the President.

14. The Treasury Secretary shall be responsible for maintaining the financial records of the Republic. He shall oversee the collection of revenue and the disbursement of payments. He shall have the power to investigate national public financial malfeasance of every kind and to arrest and indict persons alleged to have made such transgressions. He shall have the sole authority to propose legislation for the purposes of tax and revenue.

---

[44] Spontaneous (snap) elections rule1. See footnotes 52, 53.
[45] Selection of executives.
[46] Note: the Majority Leader is the Head of *Government*; the President is the Head of *State.*

15. The Attorney General shall be responsible for faithfully upholding the laws passed by the Legislature. He shall have the power to investigate national crimes of every kind except for those delegated to the Treasury, and to arrest and indict persons alleged to have made such transgressions. He shall offer non-binding advice to local peace officers and judiciaries as necessary[47].

16. Likewise, the Shadow Government shall from among their number choose the same: A Minority Leader, a Shadow Home Secretary, a Shadow Foreign Secretary, and a Shadow Attorney General. These Delegates shall have especial duty to advise their opposite numbers and present legislation to those men for consideration[48].

17. There shall be four, and only four Committees for the purpose of proposing, writing and submitting Bills to the Majority Leader. These committees shall be named Committee A, Committee B, Committee C, and Committee D. Of those Delegates in Government but not yet deputized, no less than 3 and no more than twelve Delegates shall be assigned to one committee and one committee only.

The Delegates for these assignments shall be chosen by the Majority Leader. The number of Delegates on each committee shall be equal to the others.

---

[47] Powers of Legislative leadership.
[48] Powers of the Shadow Government.

The assignment of Delegates to committees among those chosen shall be done by lot[49].

18. Any Committee may submit Legislation to the Majority Leader, the rules of this process to be determined by the whole House at the start of that year's business, before the first bill is to be considered.

When a Committee delivers a bill to the Majority Leader, he shall decide whether to submit the bill to a vote of Ratification or to table it, and set the time and conditions for that vote[50].

19. Finally, the whole body of Delegates shall vote for one of their number who is not otherwise deputized in any role enumerated above to be deputized Speaker of the House. He shall then serve as president of the House. His role is to maintain proper order and observe time and rules for the House's proceedings. He shall not have a vote on any matter except in the instance of an otherwise tie vote[51].

20. When voting on Legislation, it is presumed that those in the Majority shall vote Yea and each member of the Shadow Government shall vote Nay. Should a member of the Majority choose to vote Nay, he shall immediately cross over to the Shadow Government until the next election[52].

---

[49] Definition and composition of legislative committees within the House.

[50] Rules defining the time and conditions of legislation.

[51] Speaker rule.

[52] Presumption of unified government; Defection rule. *Note: as more votes happen during a term, more Delegates will pass into the minority. A Government without the majority results in dissolution and a spontaneous election.*

21. At any time, should the Government lose its majority, it shall end and a new election shall be held per Art. I, Section II, Clause 9[53].

22. At any time, the Majority Leader, Minority Leader or Speaker may call for a vote to dissolve the current government and hold a new election. Upon the agreement of 2/3 of the entire House, such an election shall be held per Art. I, Section II, Clause 9[54].

23. The House of Delegates shall have sole power of Impeachment, by 3/5 vote of the whole Chamber, over all elected or appointed officials in the national Government, all national Judges and the appointees of the same, including members of its own Chamber[55].

Part III. The Senate

1. The Senate shall be chosen by the several local legislatures sitting in city or county governance, and shall serve at the leisure of their appointing body and in times of good behavior. They shall not be replaced by their appointing bodies in the same one-year legislative term as that in which they were last appointed[56].

2. Each city is entitled to send two Senators, and each county, less any included city, may also send up to two Senators[57].

---

[53] Spontaneous (Snap) elections rule 2. See footnotes 43. 53.
[54] Spontaneous (Snap) election rule 3. See footnotes, 43, 52.
[55] The power of Impeachment.
[56] Indirect appointment of Senators.
[57] Definition of Senate districts. *Note: this may result in an extraordinary number of Senators.*

3. Senators must be male citizens who have reached the age of thirty and have lived domestically for the prior eight years or longer[58].

4. Each Senator shall have his primary residence within the borders of his District, and make convenient accommodations to meet with his constituents there regularly throughout the year[59].

5. The Senate shall choose from among its number and officer called the Senate President Pro Tempore, who shall serve in the same roles as the Speaker of the House of Delegates.

6. The Senate shall be subject to its own rules, voted on by the whole body at the beginning of the legislative year, prior to considering legislation.

The Senate shall choose its other officers per its own rules.

7. The Senate shall have the sole power to try all Impeachments; and by a 3/5 vote, may remove any person so Impeached.

Sanction in cases of impeachment shall not extend further than removal from office and a disqualification from further civil service. It shall not substitute for any subsequent civil or criminal trial stemming from the same circumstances[60].

8. The Senate shall have no power to Legislate. However, it shall have the power of Advice and Consent to that legislation which is

---

[58] Requirements to be a Senator.
[59] Local meeting rule, as per Art I Part II Rule 5
[60] The power to try those Impeachments referred from the House of Delegates.

passed by the House of Delegates. The Senate may as it chooses debate and amend legislation and send it back to the House for consideration. Should the House then pass the legislation again, the Senate shall send the legislation on to the President.

9. The Senate shall have the power of Advice and Consent for the heads of civil service branches appointed by the Majority Leader or by the President. It may reject any such nominee with a 3/5 vote.

10. The Senate shall have the ultimate authority to judge the Constitutionality of a law or other government act upon petition by an affected party[61].

11. The Senate shall serve as the court of first resort in disputes between polities. It may delegate this responsibility to such courts as it may establish[62].

Part IV. Elections

1. Candidates for the House of Delegates stand for election in their respective districts as described in I. II. 1-6.

2. The standard Election Day for the House and the Presidency shall be the First Tuesday after the First Monday in November, and the term of the House shall be five years, beginning on 7 January of the following calendar year.

---

[61] Supreme Constitutional Authority rule. *Note: the Senate does not get to decide by fiat, but must accept petition from some party with standing.*

[62] All courts deciding disputes which happen in more than one locality shall be created by the Senate.

Spontaneous elections called by the House membership shall not interfere with these Election Days, nor postpone them in any way. Would a spontaneous election and government formation period overlap this day, a spontaneous election shall instead not occur[63].

3. All Elections shall be held in their entirety on one day, including the submitting of secret ballots and the public counting thereof, but otherwise by rules set by each locality[64].

4. Suffrage shall be limited to male Heads of Household in each family, who are over the age of 21, and who own in whole or part their own land, and domicile thereon. These suffragers shall declare their residence at times appointed by the several local legislatures, but no sooner than six months prior to a vote.

These voters shall vote only in the district in which they so declare, and at convenient places decided by their local legislature[65],

Part V. Powers and Duties of the Houses.

1. 3/4 of The Government and 1/4 of the Shadow Government shall be sufficient to do business in the House of Delegates. A simple majority shall be sufficient to do business in the Senate[66].

---

[63] Election Day.
[64] Speedy Elections rule. *Note: there is no provision for mail ballots of any kind.*
[65] Defines suffrage for Legislative elections.
[66] Quorum rule.

2. Each House shall determine the rules of its proceedings beyond those outlined above. These rules shall be presented and voted upon at the start of the Legislative Term, after the Government is formed, but before business may be considered. Such rules shall be recorded in a Journal to be held by the Speaker or President Pro Tempore respectively and available to all Legislators.

Each House shall have the agency to punish its own Members. Each House may expel a member without Impeachment with both a vote of 2/3, and the consent of the Speaker or President Pro Tempore[67].

3. Each House shall keep an extensive and detailed Journal of its proceedings for public oversight[68].

4. No legislative actions, nor speech and debate held upon the floors of Chambers, shall be held in secret or otherwise made privileged; nor shall votes be held in other places[69].

5. Votes shall be taken publicly, with Yeas, Nays, and in the case of those not present or for those Senators abstaining, Not Voting (N.V.) recorded for each Legislator. No voice votes or unanimous consent decrees shall be allowed[70].

---

[67] Parliamentary rules.

[68] Records rule.

[69] Freedom of information rule. *Note: the secrecy required by some circumstances will require the delegation of decision-making to parties outside the Legislature.*

[70] Public vote rule.

6. Neither House may adjourn to other places to conduct business in whole or in part. All votes must be taken in person in the appointed Chamber[71].

Part VI. Legislative Process

1. Legislation shall originate in the House. It shall go to the Senate for a period of debate, followed by Advice given by the Senate to the House. The House shall then consider the notes and amendments to the legislation suggested by the Senate and make such changes as it deems necessary. The legislation then goes back to the Senate for review and on to the President for Consent[72].

2. The Senate has the privilege of unlimited debate upon first considering such legislation. Upon second review, it has five days (Less Sundays) to deliver the legislation to the President[73].

3. The President then consents to the legislation within five days (less Sundays) by signing his name to it and returning it to the House of Delegates.

The legislation, so ratified, becomes law[74].

4. Should the President refuse to sign, the legislation shall be returned to the House of Delegates immediately. It shall become law upon a 3/5 vote of the entire House[75].

---

[71] In-Person voting rule.
[72] The House of Delegates *legislates;* The Senate *advises.*
[73] Filibuster Rule.
[74] Presidential consent rule.
[75] The "weak veto" rule.

Part VII. Powers of the Legislature[76].

1. The Government shall have the power to lay and collect taxes, duties, tariffs, and other standard fees in order to pay for such costs the Republic shall incur; however all such revenue laws shall be uniform through all places and apply equally to all persons without exception. These laws and the revenue generated shall be managed by the Treasury Secretary[77];

2. To borrow money and produce bonds to cover expenses the Republic shall incur[78];

3. To write rules for international commerce and inter-district commerce[79];

4. To establish a uniform rule of Naturalization, including strict tests for cultural compatibility and suitable economic value to the Republic[80];

5. To establish banking and financial rules, and to establish a publicly-held central bank with records to be available for public review[81];

6. To produce legal tender, to regulate the value thereof internally and in relation to foreign currency[82];

---

[76] Note: there is no authority to establish a Post Office.
[77] Authority to tax; equal taxation.
[78] Authority to borrow.
[79] Delegation of international trade powers.
[80] Naturalization authority.
[81] Central bank authority; continuous audit provision.
[82] Authority to mint.

7. To fix standards of weights and measures as are customarily in use;

8. To maintain the one official language and other forms of analogous communication of the Republic[83];

9. To establish and enforce patent and copyright[84];

10. To provide funds for the establishment of the general defense excluding standard domestic armies[85];

11. To provide revenue to meet the needs of other enumerated powers; however each such bill shall provide for one and only one such need[86];

12. To make law in the following legal areas: Adoption and Family law; Antitrust and Tort; Banking and Bankruptcy; Bioethics and Medical Ethics; Commercial Law and Incorporation; Communications; Consumer Protection; Cultural Enforcement; Farm, Mining and Productive Land Usage; Prohibited and Vicious Substances (food and drug); Transportation including roads, oceans and vehicles; Space; Tax and Revenue; and Use of Common Resources on Public Land (water, grazing rights, etc.)

Being that it is imperative that a free people understand the laws under which they live and work, in each of these sectors of law, no

---

[83] Presumes a standard language and authorizes the maintenance of it.
[84] Authority to establish a Patent Office.
[85] Authority to fund the military.
[86] Prohibition on omnibus bills.

more than 100 laws shall be in effect. Furthermore, each law, when written in plain layman's language, shall not exceed 5,000 words.

No law or statute shall be passed whereby the total number of laws in a given chapter is greater than 100, or that the total words in that chapter exceed 50,000[87].

13. The Senate shall have the power to establish and oversee such Courts and Tribunals it should deem necessary to adjudicate the above matters[88].

14. The Senate shall have the power to ratify treaties agreed upon by the President by a vote of 3/5 of the Chamber[89].

Part VIII. Powers Denied the Legislature.

1. Habeas Corpus shall not be suspended for any reason whatsoever[90].

2. No Person shall be detained for longer than 40 days plus Sundays for any reason, nor shall the Legislature allow localities to make such detentions[91].

3. No bill of attainder or ex post facto law shall be passed.

4. No direct revenue law shall be enacted unless in proportion to the Census or Enumeration per Art I, Part II, Section 4[92].

---

[87] Limits legal complexity.
[88] Authorizes the Senate to establish law courts.
[89] The Senate must authorize all negotiated Treaties.
[90] Prohibits detention without due process.
[91] Prohibits lengthy detention.
[92] Prohibits income taxes and national taxes based on spending, consumption, etc. *This provision is meant to protect local governments' taxing power compared to the national*

5. No tariff or duty shall be levied on internal trade[93].

6. No tax or duty shall be levied on internal vehicular transport of goods or people, nor shall people be barred from traveling from one locality to another except by sanction in criminal court. Private fees are allowed[94].

7. No monies shall be drawn from the Treasury except by official legal appropriation to cover expenses associated with lawful action[95].

8. No Title of Nobility shall be granted by the Second Republic; And no Person holding any Office of Profit or Trust under them, shall, without the Consent of the Congress, accept of any present, Emolument, Office, or Title, of any kind whatever, from any King, Prince, or foreign State[96].

9. The Legislature, in whole or in part, shall not raise its own military forces. This task falls to the President and the several localities. It may endow such civilian offices as it deems necessary for maintaining the peace within its body and immediate grounds[97].

10. The Legislature shall not establish a national peace officer force. The responsibility for keeping the peace shall devolve upon the several localities[98].

---

government.

[93] Free commerce rule.

[94] Free movement rule.

[95] Prohibits black budgets.

[96] National fidelity rule.

[97] Rule prohibiting the Legislature from establishing its own military separate from the President's apparatus.

[98] Rule prohibiting national or secret police.

11. No legislative business of any kind shall occur on Sunday. For the purposes of counting days (e.g. Art. I. I. 8,) Sunday is not counted.

Part IX. Powers Denied to Localities.

1. No locality, be it city, county or otherwise, shall enter into any act of foreign policy or confederation with another locality[99].

2. No locality shall mint money except by permission of the Government[100].

3. No locality, without consent of the Government, shall lay duties or tariffs on imports or exports except to cover the expense of inspection. The net revenue from such levies shall go to the Treasury of the Republic. All such local laws shall be subject to review and revision by the Senate[101].

4. No locality shall raise an army except for the purpose of training the militia, nor keep a standing army or other official military force. Instead they shall raise civilian peace officers, sheriffs and bailiffs as they find necessary to maintain the peace. At such time as a locality has been invaded or infiltrated by a foreign entity, it is entitled to use whatever force necessary to repel the attack and subdue the enemy[102].

---

[99] The national government is solely responsible for foreign policy.
[100] The national government controls the mint.
[101] The national government sets international trade policy.
[102] The national government regulates military action within the country's borders.

5. No Person shall be detained for longer than 40 days plus Sundays for any reason, nor shall the Legislature allow localities to make such detentions.

Article II. The President.

Part I. Definition.

1. The Powers of Head of State, Head of the Military, and Chief Diplomat shall be vested in an office of the President of the Second Republic.

Part II. Qualifications.

1. The President must be a male citizen who has reached the age of forty and has lived domestically for the prior five years or longer. Any candidate for this office must be born within its borders or have been a citizen since the founding of the State, and have never relinquished or lost his citizenship.

Part III. Electing the President.

1. The President shall hold his Office during the Term of Five Years, and be elected as follows[103].

2. Each House District shall hold a direct election for President among its suffragers on the same day as its own five-year term election. This day is the First Tuesday after the First Monday in

---

[103] The Presidential term of office coincides with the House's General Elections.

November. This election shall result in delegating that district's authority to one Presidential Elector.

3. On the same day, each locality which may send Senators to the Senate shall choose, in a manner decided by its Legislature, one Presidential Elector.

4. Ten days after these selections (excluding Sundays), all Electors shall meet in the House Chamber and cast one vote for President. The man who receives the most Electoral Votes shall assume the Office of the Presidency at noontime on January 7th following[104].

Part IV. The Vice-President.

1. Upon his election in Chambers, the President shall choose a Vice-President who must fulfil the same requirements as those for the President. This Vice-President shall act as chief advisor to the President during his term. Should the President be unable to fulfil his duties, the Vice-President shall serve as President temporarily or until the end of the current presidential term[105].

Part V. Powers And Responsibilities of the President.

1. The President shall be the chief representative of the Republic to the world. He shall serve as the Delegate of the whole of the people and advocate for its welfare and advancement among the people and nations of the world[106].

---

[104] The Electoral College.
[105] The Vice President is an advisor not subject to Senatorial oversight.
[106] The President is the Head of State.

2. The President is the Chief Diplomat of the Republic. He shall meet with the highest Officers of other states and entities on behalf of the people. He shall have the power to negotiate treaties and alliances subject to the ratification of the Senate. He shall be the Head of the Foreign Service and in this role work closely with the Foreign Secretary[107].

3. The President shall be the Commander-In-Chief of the Republic's military. He shall have the power to Declare War. He shall have the power to disburse those funds allocated by the House to any military project besides a standing Army[108].

4. Being necessary for a defense of the borders and interior of our Republic, the President, as he determines, shall construct a Navy, which may include an Air Force, Space Force and Marine force. The Navy shall operate at the several ports and in the open seas.

He shall also construct a Domestic Corps of Engineers. This Corps is designated as part of the military. It shall support such martial forces as are deemed necessary. The Corps shall be responsible for maintenance and logistics of such facilities and equipment which may be needed for the domestic defense in times of war, including dual-use infrastructure such as highways, canals and shelters[109].

---

[107] The President is the chief diplomat.

[108] The President is the head of the military. *Note: In the American system, Congress funds the military and declares war, while the President commands the troops. In this system, the House funds the military, but the President forms it, heads it and declares war.*

[109] Describes the general makeup of the military. *Note: there is no standing army.*

5. The President shall have the power, in times of war, to call upon the several local militias, for a period of time appropriate, for the national defense. This muster shall be taken with the Advice of local militia leaders, but the ultimate authority is vested in the Office of the President[110].

6. The President has the responsibility to personally Commission all military officers of the Republic[111].

7. The House shall provide the President a suitable allowance for administering to his office and duties. He shall choose the staff to hire and this staff serves at his pleasure[112].

8. The President shall appoint a number of Chief Officers to assist him in the Administration of his several tasks. The Senate must Advise, and then Consent, by a simple majority vote, prior to these appointments. These Officers shall serve at the pleasure of the President. Among these officers shall be a Secretary of War and a Secretary of Foreign Affairs[113].

The President shall have the power to Commission such Officers to fill Vacancies which may occur during the recess of the Senate, to expire at the end of that Legislative Session[114].

---

[110] Authority to muster volunteer forces.
[111] The President establishes military rank and hierarchy and must approve all officers.
[112] Privilege of administration offices.
[113] Department heads will be political appointees subject to Senate consent.
[114] The recess appointment rule. *Note: No recess appointee may serve longer than the rest of the calendar year before gaining Senate approval.*

9. He shall present to the Republic, from time to time, an Address on the State of the Republic, and recommend for the House's consideration such measures as he shall judge to be necessary and expedient. This Address may be in the form of a Speech or in writing[115].

10. Each House shall grant its members one recess of at least 30 consecutive days each year, and must convene for at least 30 days each year. If either House shall wish to adjourn more than once or adjourn on a short notice, the President shall have the power to refuse such irregular order[116].

11. The President shall have the power to grant Pardon, Clemency or Reprieve to any person or citizen convicted of a crime, but not to grant Immunity against future criminal convictions[117].

12. The President shall receive no salary or compensation for his services. Instead he shall receive a Per Diem of 1% of the average national wages, and be permitted to use the President's residence as defined by the House of Delegates without charge. As with the Legislatures, his wealth shall be held in blind trust during his service[118].

As Chief Diplomat and Head of State, he shall be entitled to use such Government facilities as his duties require. As Head of the

---

[115] Requires a State of the Republic address.
[116] Prevents one part of the Legislature from fleeing chambers to prevent a quorum and thereby blocking legislation.
[117] The power of Pardon stems from Sovereign Authority under English Common Law.
[118] The President's compensation.

Military, he shall be entitled to use such Military conveyances as his duties require for both war and peacetime activity[119].

Part VI. Impeachment and Removal.

1. In times of bad behavior, the Legislature may Impeach and Remove from office the President and Vice-President as per their usual procedures.

2. Should either man be convicted of Vote Fraud, Bribery, Counterfeiting, Piracy or Treason, that man shall be subject to immediate Impeachment and Trial[120].

Article III. The Judiciary.

Part I. Investiture.

1. The National judicial power of the Republic shall be vested in the Senate, as described in I. III. 10.

2. The Senate shall establish, by its own authority, such inferior courts as it may deem necessary[121].

3. This national court or system of courts shall not interfere with local courts, sheriffs, bailiffs, justices of the peace, courts or

---

[119] The President's perquisites.

[120] What constitutes bad behavior is left to the Legislature. The second clause implies that the Presidents are subject to criminal penalty.

[121] The authority to establish courts for disputes above a local level is vested in the Senate.

tribunals of any kind, but may upon its authority accept appeals from parties having previously been subject to lower court rulings[122].

4. Justices and other officers of the court shall receive Compensation for their public service not greater than the average national wage from two years prior[123].

5. The Senate shall give license to localities to establish petty courts and tribunals to dispense with disputes of local importance and to adjudicate local laws and disputes as the need shall arise. These courts shall be inferior to the National courts[124].

Part II. Scope.

1. Judicial power shall extend to All Cases in Law and Equity as well as civil matters as they pertain to the Laws of the Republic. Those National courts shall not judge cases based on local law; however at their discretion, the Senate may pass judgement on the Constitutionality of any laws in any case. The Senate must be petitioned by an aggrieved party and then accept the petition prior to deliberating on a given law's constitutionality[125].

2. All criminal actions shall be tried by a Jury of 12 Citizens over the age of 18 and presided over by a Judge, unless the parties to the case agree to some other method of trial. Civil actions may be tried

---

[122] Implies existence of local courts.
[123] Judicial compensation.
[124] Authorizes local courts; the word "license" means that the Senate must approve them.
[125] Constitutional oversight.

in a manner amenable to both parties in the suit or by a Jury of six Citizens over the age of 18 and presided over by a Judge[126].

3. Courts shall have the power of Judicial Review and Interpretation. Where a law is ambivalent, it is incumbent upon the Court to decide its meaning and write its decision and reasoning in the writ of decision[127].

4. Juries shall have the power of Statutory Review. Should a jury find a law unjust, it is their duty to find for the defendant and state the reason for such finding to be the unjust law in question. Such laws shall be considered by the Senate for review and possible repeal from time to time[128].

Part III. Limits.

1. As those Persons who have been incarcerated for correction, and then released, seldom improve as Citizens, The Institution of Secure Correction shall be forbidden. Defendants may still be held prior to trial at the discretion of the Court for up to 40 days plus Sundays. Alternatively, a Court may set cash bail and release a defendant awaiting trial or sentencing with written conditions attached[129].

2. Felony conviction shall result in loss of citizenship and immediate exile.

---

[126] Right to Trial by Jury.
[127] Authorizes judicial statutory review.
[128] Authorizes jury nullification.
[129] Limited detention rule. Cash bail rule.

3. Misdemeanor conviction shall result in a fine and restitution paid to the aggrieved party.

As alternative to restitution available to the indigent shall be probation and parole for a fixed period defined by statute; additional offenses during this probationary period shall result in penalties per a felony conviction[130].

4. Laws shall be interpreted broadly with wide scope rather than narrowly. Legal arguments shall progress from the specific to the general and not vice-versa[131].

5. Laws shall be made and enforced at the most local level possible. Should a court find that a national law is unsuitable for its locality, it shall petition the Senate to overturn such a law on Constitutional grounds[132].

6. Laws shall be written and enforced equally across all citizens, including any government Officers. Should a court find that a law is written in a manner to be unequally applied, it shall petition the Senate to overturn such a law on Constitutional grounds. No law shall exempt those who legislate, execute or adjudicate laws[133].

---

[130] Establishes punishments for Felonies and Misdemeanors.

[131] Principle of Broad Interpretation. This rule should mitigate the ability for jurists to whittle a law down to nothing, for instance in the case of the U.S. Second Amendment.

[132] Principle of Local Primacy. This rule should mitigate the power of the national government to dominate localities.

[133] Principle of Equal Application. Laws must contain no exemptions, just as laws may not Attainder one individual or group.

7. Laws shall be written in simple, contemporary language accessible to laymen. Should a court find a law which is unnecessarily complicated or incomprehensible, that court shall petition the Senate to overturn that law on Constitutional grounds[134].

8. Given that language and the meaning of words and phrases will change over time, the court shall endeavor to interpret law based on its original meaning rather than based on the language's meaning in its own time and place[135].

9. Besides the Senate, no more than one-half of Judges at each level may be members of the Bar or be trained primarily in Law. The remainder must be male citizens over 21 with some militia service[136].

Part IV. Enumerated Laws.

1. These following laws, so enumerated, are not subject to statutory or judicial review, nor to correction by any means whatever besides Amendment of this Document.

2. Treason against the Second Republic shall consist only in levying war against them, or in adhering to their enemies, giving them aid and comfort.

---

[134] Principle of Simple Language. Men should be able to understand the laws by which they are governed.

[135] Principle of Originalism. This rule should mitigate the drift in meaning over time.

[136] Out of all government officials, judges are unique in that they are drawn from the ranks of a very narrow class of people. This rule intends to mitigate that dilemma.

The Congress shall have power to declare the punishment of treason, but no attainder of treason shall work corruption of blood, or forfeiture except during the life of the person attained.

3. Counterfeiting legal tender of the Second Republic shall consist only in creating documents, bills, notes coinage and other tokens of value for the purpose of legerdemain, fraud, or bypass of the lawful money system[137].

Digital currencies and other financial products which are not tied to any country or bank shall be legal, but shall not be legal tender for the purposes of Government custom[138].

4. Piracy of Second Republican flagged vessels shall be punishable by exile.

5. Vote Fraud, Conspiracy to Commit Vote Fraud and any Accessory to Vote Fraud against the Second Republic of any kind shall result in forfeiture of all assets and immediate exile. Furthermore the person so convicted shall be barred from return to this soil in perpetuity[139].

6. This Constitution in total shall expire upon the last day of the calendar year 40 years after the year of its Ratification.

---

[137] Personal or corporate bonds and other investment vehicles shall be legal, as regulated by the Legislature.

[138] Punishments for Counterfeiting shall be set by the Legislature. They shall not be less than a fine equal to the money so Counterfeited.

[139] Of all crimes, vote fraud shall be judged to be the worst of all.

Article IV. The Civil Service.

Part I. Definition.

1. "Civil Service" shall mean any job or office of honor, within any level of government, whether compensated or uncompensated, aside from those positions which are Military in nature. This rule shall be adjudicated broadly in times of Dilemma.

Part II. Limitations.

1. Civil servants of every kind and at every level of government shall serve no longer than twenty years in total. This includes all Officers as well as tradesmen and craftsmen. Military Service shall not be so limited[140].

2. Only Citizens shall hold any position in the Civil Service.

3. Civil service unions, for the purpose of collective bargaining and for the purpose of any political activity whatsoever, shall be strictly prohibited. Public unions of these kinds are also prohibited[141].

4. Civil servants and their families shall be strictly prohibited from political advocacy or giving, to another person or cause, during their tenure. They may still stand for public Office and in this capacity accept advocacy from non-prohibited groups[142].

---

[140] This rule introduces firm term limits and limits the ability of bureaucracy to become professionalized.

[141] This rule bans government unions.

[142] This rule bans civil servants from other kinds of political action.

5. No civil servant may earn, in total compensation per year, more than the national average salary paid to heads of household two years prior[143].

Article V. Pertaining to Liberty and Union.

Part I. Full Faith and Credit.

1. Full faith and credit shall be given in each locality to the public acts, records and judicial proceedings of every other locality. Any licensure or criminal sanction shall be honored across these lines. The enforcement of such shall fall upon the several local peace officers as directed by the Attorney General.

Part II. Reciprocal License and Liberty.

1. The citizens of each locality shall have the same privileges and immunities as all other citizens.

2. Whenever a person charged with a crime in one jurisdiction is found in another, the Executive of the originating jurisdiction may order the fugitive returned.

Part III. Enforcing the Union.

1. No locality may invade or occupy another; nor shall it invade or occupy other lands without consent of the President. The President

---

[143] This rule limits salary.

may call, as is needed, any and all militia into service to repel such insult and secure the welfare of the citizenry and lands.

2. No City or County shall be founded, nor shall a City or County secede from another, without the prior consent of the national Government and the Senate, with a simple majority vote in each Chamber[144].

3. The President shall guarantee each locality a Representative form of government, whether it be a Mayor, a Mayor-Council, Council, Plebiscite, or other form of republican rule as determined by that locality's charter[145].

Article VI. Amendments to This Regime.

Part I. By The People.

1. At any time, should 2/3 of localities pass a referendum agreeing to specific Amendment of this Constitution, the Constitution shall be so Amended at the start of the next national legislative session on 7 January, and such Amendment shall be added to this Constitution.

2. At any time, should 2/3 of local legislatures pass a Constitutional Resolution agreeing to specific Amendment of this Constitution, the Constitution shall be so Amended at the start of the next national

---

[144] This rule should prevent packing the Senate.
[145] A Plebiscite is a town meeting form of government.

legislative session on 7 January, and such Amendment shall be added to this Constitution[146].

---

[146] There is no time limit for these ratifications.

Part III. By The House.

1. The National Legislature, whenever 2/3 of both Houses shall deem it necessary, shall propose Amendment to this Constitution. And should 3/4 of the Local Legislatures affirm this proposal, the Constitution shall be so Amended at the start of the next national legislative session on 7 January, and such Amendment shall be added to this Constitution[147].

Part IV. By Convention.

1. During any calendar year, should 3/4 of Localities, by referendum of the People so declare, there shall be a Constitutional Convention held in the Chambers of the Legislatures prior to the start of the next Legislative Year.

2. Such Convention shall begin on 6 January at 12 Noon and continue for as long as necessary. Only after this Convention shall the Houses meet.

3. Each Locality is entitled to send three Representatives to this Convention and to pay them per diems as the local legislature deems appropriate.

4. No person who has been employed in the civil service for the last 8 years shall be entitled to serve as Representative.

---

[147] There is no time limit for these ratifications.

5. No person who is not a Citizen shall be entitled to serve as Representative.

6. No Person not registered to vote in his Locality shall be entitled to serve as Representative.

7. Attendees shall set the rules for the Convention.

8. The purpose of this convention is to Propose and Vote on changes to this Constitution. Such changes as Ratified shall be binding.

9. At the expiration of this Regime, per Art. III Part IV Section 6, such a Constitutional Convention shall commence per the rules listed above. In the interim, the Legislature shall be Dissolved and Government shall be continued by the Civil Service and the President.

Article VII. Ratification.

1. Ratification by Convention of 2/3 of Localities shall be sufficient to immediately enact this Constitution.

Appendix IV. Specific Prohibitions.

The following are the first eleven prohibitions against the Regime's powers, enshrined in the Constitution, listed after the final Article, and are intended to protect individual rights.

Any further amendments to the Constitution shall, along with these prohibitions, be referred to as A Gathering of Rights. However, they are also the responsibilities of every man to keep them.

First Prohibition.

This document enumerates specific prohibitions against government action. These Prohibitions enshrine and ratify individual rights granted by God and belonging inalienably to each Person. These specific prohibitions against government actions shall not be taken to mean that the individual rights so protected are the only rights a person possesses. Personal Liberty is expansive, while Government insult against those rights shall be as minimal as possible.

Second Prohibition.

The Government shall make no law abridging the practice of Christianity or regarding the means, times and places thereof.

Third Prohibition.

Section 1

The Government shall make no law abridging freedom of speech
and shall protect such freedom to speak in the Public Square,
whether in person, online, or in other spheres, regardless of
whether those spaces are public or private.

Section 2

As the Press is the whole of the People, the Government shall make
no law abridging freedom to publish, and shall treat the written
word with the same weight as the spoken word for the purposes of
such protections as defined above.

Fourth Prohibition.

The Government shall make no law abridging the People's right to
peaceably assemble. Nor shall it prevent or inhibit Citizens from
petitioning their Delegates and other public officials for a redress of
their grievances by any peaceful means.

Fifth Prohibition.

The State shall not prevent or inhibit through any law or regulation
any Citizen from owning and maintaining any arms or weapons
possessed by the State, including weapons of war. If the State may
own such a device, so may any Citizen.

Sixth Prohibition.

Section 1

As pursuit of property and ownership and homesteading of a
domicile is essential to a person's liberty and security, the State
shall not seize or occupy any private property by force or
subterfuge. No private property shall be forfeited through legal
action prior to conviction, though it may be held by the State during
any period of incarceration.

Section 2

No private property shall be taken by the State for any reason
without just compensation.

Seventh Prohibition.

Section 1

The right of the people to be secure in the persons, houses, papers
and effects, whether physical or digital, and against both public and
private scrutiny, shall not be violated. A person has absolute right
and authority over his own information. The Government and
private companies shall afford privacy to the owner such property
so long as there is a reasonable assumption of privacy, even if in fact
there is no privacy. This means, among other things, online
correspondence and speech from a position of anonymity shall be
held as private.

Section 2

Should the Government have reasonable suspicion of criminal activity, it may seek a public Warrant from a judge in the appropriate jurisdiction supported by written affidavit, and present such warrant to the person or entity subject to that search, prior to the search, detailing the reasons for the search, the places to be searched, and the evidence or person sought.

Eighth Prohibition.

Section 1

No Person shall be held to answer for a Felony unless first indicted by a Grand Jury, except in cases arising from military action or service; nor shall any person be subject to prosecution more than once for crimes stemming from any circumstance or incident; nor shall any person be compelled to testify against himself, his household, a medical patient, or in the case of a priest or pastor, against a person who has confessed to him in the context of religious sacrament or consultation.

Section 2

No Person shall be deprived of any property, right, privilege or benefit without due process of law.

Ninth Prohibition.

Section 1

No Person shall be held in custody for longer than 40 days, plus Sundays, for any reason.

Section 2

In all criminal prosecutions, the accused shall enjoy the right to a speedy and public trial, by an impartial jury of the State and district wherein the crime shall have been committed, which district shall have been previously ascertained by law, and to be informed of the nature and cause of the accusation; to be confronted with the witnesses against him; to have compulsory process for obtaining witnesses in his favor, and to have the assistance of counsel for his defense.

Section 3

Excessive bail shall not be required, nor excessive fines imposed, nor cruel and unusual punishments inflicted. Those punishments inflicted shall be determined by statute. Should there be no statutory punishment, the punishment shall be determined by a jury; or if no jury is present, by the presiding officer.

Section 4

In civil suits, the right of trial by jury shall not be abridged, and the court costs shall be paid by the loser of such a suit. Should the suit utilize public court accommodations, and the parties settle before a judgement is reached, the parties shall split the cost of the public accommodations equally.

Tenth Prohibition.

Those powers not enumerated and delegated to the State in this document are reserved for localities or for the Citizenry.

Eleventh Prohibition.

Laws shall be written in their entirety by the Government and not delegated to unelected persons or agencies to write in the form of regulation.

# # #